Memory Tools

Memory Tools

by Graham Old

Techniques to maximise your memory
for therapists, teachers and trainers

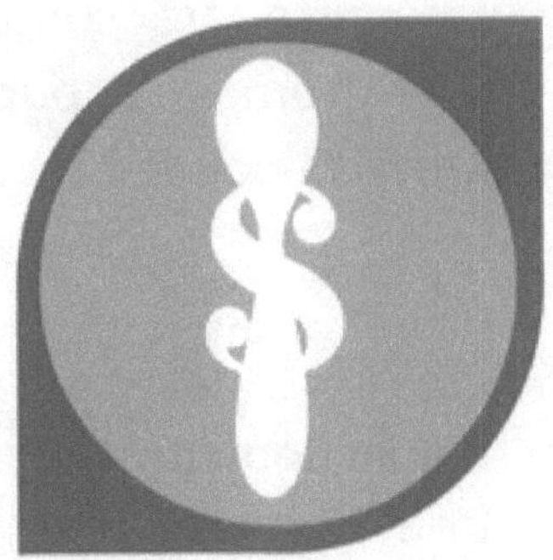

Memory Tools

Copyright © GRAHAM OLD

First published 2020 by Plastic Spoon

Acknowledgements

With thanks to Richard Nongard and the ICBCH for tirelessly working to raise the standard of hypnosis training, networking, practice and reputation. This has all been done with a spirit of generosity and camaraderie that is without equal.

In memory of Tony Buzan and in gratitude for the many years he spent advocating for effective learning techniques, memory improvement and mind sports.

Contents

Introduction

In the year 2000, I was just about to enter the 3rd year of my Theology degree. I had been fortunate enough to have developed a rather all-consuming interest in the human memory a few years earlier, which was proving to be useful for my studies.

One thing lead to another and – at a time in my life when I had much better things to be doing - I found myself sat in a large hall at Alexander Palace in London, surrounded by a few dozen fellow competitors, taking part in the World Memory Championships. I did not win. I did not even close! However, I came 8th, which is a better result than I had expected. It no longer really gets me bragging rights, but I am still fairly pleased with it all these years later.

My most successful event was the Poem, where we had 15 minutes to read a poem and recall as much as possible, including punctuation, line-breaks, capital letters and so on.[1] I came 4th in that event, but the most significant thing for me is that I beat the reigning World Champion and a number of the top ranked 'mentathletes' in the world.

Fast forward a couple of decades and I now find myself in a field that heavily relies upon the use of words. Some therapists use entire scripts that they read to their clients, making perhaps only minor changes and customisations along the way. I sometimes need to remember the names of numerous phobias, or the order in which to carry out a particular therapeutic process, recall a client's spouse, their children's names, their age or important events in their life.

So, I am now grateful that my geeky teenage self used to spend hours in the local library learning techniques that would prove to be useful time and time again. It is my hope that you also will find the following information beneficial, both personally and professionally.

Nothing that follows is original to me. Absolutely nothing. All I have done is collate systems, methods and techniques that I have proven to be effective and found ways to apply them to tasks frequently required of

---

1   The Poem event was later removed from the WMC due to the increasing number of competitors for whom English was a second language.

MEMORY TOOLS

therapists, teachers, trainers and other helpers.

GRAHAM OLD

Association

When someone learns anything new, no matter what the subject-matter, it is always learned and remembered through association with familiar knowledge.[2]

Let's get straight to it!

The first thing you need to know is that there is *nothing* more important to memorising data than association. In practical terms, we remember a new piece of information by associating it to something we have already memorised. We effectively make it possible to remember something by connecting it in some way to something that we already have 'stored' in our memory banks.[3]

We can see this easily if we consider a series of numbers:

---

2   P. 58. *The Practical Way to a Better Memory*, Bruno Furst,

3   The idea of 'storing' something in our memories is a completely inaccurate explanation for how the human memory works. However, as an analogy, it serves our current needs well enough.

206631880710739731117

Displayed in such a way, the prospect of recalling that 21-digit number may seem highly unlikely. After all, what exactly is memorable about 9731117? To remember this intimidating number, we need to associate it with something we already know. Here are some quick examples that occur to me immediately.

One number that leaps out to me, as an Englishman, is 66. That's because I know 1966 is the year that England last won the World Cup. (I'm talking about Soccer, for all of you US Americans!) It also makes me think of the 66 books which make up the Bible. However, before we even get to that, 20 is the year (and century) that this book is being written in.

31 was the number of my childhood home that got destroyed in a fire. There are two 8s in that sequence, which might make me think of Snowmen, or the rather insulting bingo call: "Two fat ladies."

07 could be seen as an obvious reference to James Bond. Number 10 is the official home of the Prime Minister in Downing Street.

73 is the year that one of my childhood heroes, Bruce

Lee, died. '97 is the year my first daughter was born. Then we have another 31.

11 – again, due to a Bingo call – makes me think of "legs eleven," so I instantly picture a ballerina. And the final 7 makes me think of the Seven Wonders of the World, so I picture a pyramid.

Whilst it may still not be clear how you would actually go about remembering this 21 digit number, I hope that it already seems slightly more manageable. We can now replace that troublesome number with the following 11 images:

- A 2020 Calendar (With the numbers written LARGE)
- Bobby Moore lifting up the World Cup
- A fire-fighter
- Two snowmen holding hands (well, branches!)
- James Bond
- The ominous black front door of 10 Downing Street
- Bruce Lee (maybe performing a flying kick?)
- My eldest daughter
- My childhood home
- A ballerina doing a pirouette
- The Great Pyramid of Giza, Egypt

Now that may still seem difficult to memorise, but it's a whole lot easier than 206631880710739731117! In fact, even without relying on the techniques that follow, I'm fairly confident that most people could recall the new list after just a few minutes of rote repetition.

However, you will soon learn that even that is not necessary. We will not look at memorising numbers until later in the book, but for now it should be fairly obvious that it is easier to remember something if you can find a connection between the thing to be memorised and something that you already know.

After all, why should 3188 be memorable? Isn't it much easier to think of a fire-fighter hosing down – and thus melting – two snowmen? And Bruce Lee flying through the air to kick my eldest daughter in the face is far easier – though less pleasant – to remember than 7397!

The 3 keys that we will be employing time and time again throughout this book are *Association*, *Imagination* and *Organisation*. You will find that once you are regularly and effectively using all three, remembering data becomes not simply easier, but natural and even fun. (Few people believe me when I tell them this, but I actually enjoyed sitting the exams for my degree, as it was simply a case of walking through a number of stories that I had devised. More on that later!) However, if we had to choose only one key out of the three, it would be association.

Let's consider a series of ten words:

Muscle

Trifle

Cactus

Kitten

Train

Painter

Ocean

Rainbow

Sausage

Clock

One of the things to note here is that if one of these words has a connection that is in some way personal to you, that is a very powerful association. For example, I am not particularly a pet person. However, if you have actually owned a kitten, you will almost certainly associate that word (which is nothing more than a two-syllable sound) with an experience you have had.

The word will likely conjure up images of your kitten, but perhaps also feelings you had for that cat and maybe some potent memories you have. It is no longer a word to be remembered, but an association you can make.

When I was growing-up, there was something of an ongoing joke that my cousin would always bring a trifle to family events. Thus, it is not simply a 6-letter word for me; it is a portal to years of memories, not least of which is the sight and sound of my cousin. If you had trifle at Christmas, you might make that association. Even if all the word does is make you think of a picture of a trifle, then you are making an association. Just think how much easier it is for you to recall that word than for a non-English speaker, who may simply hear the sound, "try full."

We might also consider how much easier this list of words would be to recall if we could somehow create extra associations *within* the list. For example, a muscle-bound man punching a bowl of trifle, a cactus pricking a kitten, or whatever the monstrosity of a "sausage clock" might be!

However, we are getting ahead of ourselves and have

already moved onto the Link Method, which is the first "Peg System" we will explore below.

GRAHAM OLD

Imagination

There is not much that needs to be said in this chapter, other than highlighting that the items that were easiest to remember – in both the 21-digit number and the list of words – were things we could imagine.

I did not simply see the number 31 and associate it with an experience from my childhood. Neither did I merely connect it to the word "fire." Instead, I converted that 2-digit number into the image of a fire-fighter. Or, I may have imagined my childhood home on fire.

As therapists, we work with words all day long. Yet, most of us recognise that the words have no impact in and of themselves. They have to *mean* something to our clients. There has to be an association between the word and something meaningful. Yet, this is not at a purely conceptual level. Words and concepts alone change no one.

Instead, through an engaged use of their imaginations, our clients connect a word to a concept and then apply that concept to their lives in some way. That is, they imagine the word and how it might be relevant to them.

You will probably have noticed that with both the numbers and words in the last chapter, I mostly converted them to people or things. This is because most of us find that using visual imagery is a more effective way of remembering something than simply thinking of a word or sound.

However, that does not mean that imagination is only about imagery. In almost all cases, a multi-sensory approach is to be preferred. As well as the sight of my childhood home on fire, I might recall the sound of the fire, the intense feeling of heat and – significantly – *how it made me feel*.

So, using our imaginations to visualise something is not the only way to remember it. For example, if we return to the two words, *Muscle* and *Trifle*, we can do more than simply picture someone punching a trifle. We might imagine the sound of their fist hitting the trifle. We might see the movement of the trifle as it splatters through the air. We might hear gasps or yelps from onlookers. We may even imagine the feeling of the trifle as it lands on our face!

It seems that I may need to take back something that

I said in the introduction. I said that there is nothing original in this book. Whilst I would still argue that such a statement is literally accurate, I am going to state something here that is not found in too many memory improvement books. However, I consider this central to my own successful efforts at memorising every day items as well as meaningless competition data. *Emotions can be just as powerful as images*.

Consider that a muscle bound man punching a trifle may not be half as memorable as the same muscle-bound man punching *your* kitten. You have an extra association – and a personal one too – so there is more emotion involved. I would therefore argue that emotion should be considered the 6th sense when it comes to using your imagination and senses to visualise and remember something.

Smashin' Scope

Tony Buzan has written more about memory than almost anyone. He popularised the useful acronym SMASHIN' SCOPE to convey the principles of effective memorisation. Each letter in the phrase refers to a way of making stronger images and associations, for the purposes of reliable recall.

Here is what the acronym represents:

- ✓ **S**ynaesthesia/Sensuality
- ✓ **M**ovement
- ✓ **A**ssociation
- ✓ **S**exuality
- ✓ **H**umour
- ✓ **I**magination
- ✓ **N**umbers

- ✓ **S**ymbolism
- ✓ **C**olour
- ✓ **O**rder and/or Sequence
- ✓ **P**ositive Images
- ✓ **E**xaggeration

Let us unpack this a little.

Synaesthesia and Sensuality

Synaesthesia refers to the use of our senses. Do not merely see an image to be remembered. The key is to use as many senses as possible, even having them interconnect in some way.

Vision - What does it look like? Colour? Brightness? Size?

Hearing - What does it sound like?

Smell - What is the smell? Pleasant? Pungent?

Taste – Is there a taste sensation? Describe it.

Touch - What does it feel like? Texture? Temperature?

Movement

Action enhances almost all memories. Make your images alive and active, as if they were scenes from a movie, rather than a snapshot. Do not simply see a still image of a man punching a trifle (or a kitten!). Make it move!

Association

As we have already discussed, what you are trying to

remember should be associated with something you already know. Make as many associations and connections as you can.

Sexuality

We almost all have a good memory and wild imagination when it comes to sex, so why not use it? Think of it this way – no one needs to know that you used strong sexual imagery to remember something.

Humour

The more ridiculous, absurd, funny and surreal you can make your images, the more memorable they will be. Additionally, humour puts your mind into a playful state making you more creative and open to new possibilities.

Imagination

Do not simply think of the item to be remembered. The more fantastic and wild the images you create in your mind can be, the more effectively they will be memorised. Let your imagination run wild and free!

Number

Numbering adds specificity and efficiency to the principle of order and sequence. We will see some benefits of this when we consider Organisation in the next chapter.

Symbolism

A picture, or so they say, is worth a thousand words. To effectively remember those 1000 words, or 1000 pieces of information, you symbolise them through imagery.

You will see this principle being used throughout the book in every example we consider. Boring, meaningless or mundane information is represented by memorable symbols and thus becomes easy to recall.

Colour

Use all the colours of the rainbow to colour your image. Unless it is intentional and for a specific reason, try not to make your associations just in black and white. Go all out and make them in full glorious technicolour!

Order (or Sequence)

When items are memorised in a sequence, this allows our brains to follow a pattern which enables recall. We can then remember the items by taking a mental journey through the sequence. You will see the true effectiveness of this when we turn to the method of Loci.

Positive Images

On the whole, we seem better at recalling happy images. When images are bright and positive we are more likely to enjoy the experience of recalling them.

However, I have to add a slight caveat here. I do not imagine that I will ever forget the image of my house on fire, or the sound of the flames, or the bustle of the fire-fighters. So, whilst this point generally stands, I would also add the sub-point that it is *emotional* images that are the really effective ones for the purposes of memorisation. Usually, you will want to make those images positive, but perhaps not always. (Still remember that poor kitten?!)

Exaggeration

This is important. As far as possible, exaggerate *everything* in your images. Exaggerate the size, action, colours, sounds and quantities. Seriously, everything! I cannot over-state this point. If I've said it once, I've said it ten thousand times: EXAGGERATE!

We will turn now to the final pillar of effective memorisation: *Organisation*. This will pave the way for us to look into some wonderfully simple yet effective memory systems. We will then move up a gear as we consider ancient and efficient memory methods and share how these can be applied to memorising scripts, processes, personal information and more.

Organisation

It is one thing to recognise that Bobby Moore lifting up the World Cup in front of a house that is burning down is more memorable than the numbers 6631. That is a valid association of those numbers with something more meaningful, utilising memorable imagery. However, how do we actually remember and – more importantly – later recall that information?

For example, I may associate 07 with James Bond, but how will I recall that it came between 88 and 10? That's where organisation comes into it.

Association and Imagination are all about making something memorable. Organisation is about how (and where) to recall that information when it is needed.

We are going to look at 3 effective and efficient ways to organise data in such a way that you can easily recall it when you need to.

These 3 ways are:

1. Linking

2. Peg Systems

3. The method of Loci (or Locations)

Some people may argue that, strictly speaking, the use of Loci is a Peg system. That may well be the case, though I would suggest it is that and a whole lot more. Nevertheless, it will be helpful for us to look at the method of loci separately.

So, without further ado, let's turn to the first means of organising data you need to remember: Linking.

Link Method

At its most simple, Linking (sometimes referred to as making chains or Chaining) creates an extra association between one or more item that you wish to recall. Then, that chain is linked to another and then another and another and so on.

Now, here's the secret: we have already begun to do this!

We associated 31 with my childhood home and then linked it to the next image (two snowmen). We associated 73 with Bruce Lee and also 97 with my daughter's birth. We then linked the four digits by picturing Bruce Lee unkindly flying through the air and kicking my daughter. In that way, we connected four individual digits together.

Additionally, we have also already done this with words. We associated "muscle" with a muscle-bound man. We next associated the word "trifle" with a childhood gathering. (At least, I did!) And we then took the extra step of linking two words by picturing a muscle-bound man punching a trifle. We could have also linked the next two words (which, in case you've forgotten them, were *cactus* and *kitten*) by picturing a cactus stabbing a kitten in the backside (because bums are always funny – and thus memorable!).

However, as an organisational strategy, that is still somewhat lacking. After all, how do we get from a man punching a trifle to a cactus stabbing a kitten? Well, as it happens, there are two approaches we could take.

We could create a completely new image, linking trifle and cactus. Then we would somehow need to link that image to the previous one (muscle + trifle) and the next one (cactus + kitten). Or we could link together what we already have. So, we either choose:

(Muscle + trifle) + (trifle + cactus) + (cactus + kitten)

Or, we opt for:

Muscle + trifle + cactus + kitten

The latter option is much more efficient and would give us a link like this:

A muscle-bound man punches a bowl of trifle during a family gathering. It splatters through the air and lands on a prized cactus, which topples over and pricks a kitten in the backside.

The kitten yelps and runs off, jumping on a child's toy train (which was inexplicably circling the room!). As the train is diverted from its usual path, it knocks over a (toy) painter who was painting an ocean on the outside of the Station.[4] His paint-brush and paints fly everywhere, leaving an impromptu rainbow on the wall.

The brushes land with a crash, causing the conductors strange "sausage clock" - a clock where the outer circle and the hands are made of various sausages, obviously – to fall off of the wall.

Here's the thing: I appreciate that such a story may sound difficult to remember, but in practice it really is not. In actual fact, you are simply remembering item 1. Item 1 then makes you recall item 2. Item 2 is linked to item 3. Item 3 immediately brings to mind item 4. And so on.

Seriously, try it now. How much of that bizarre story can you remember?

---

4   You have naturally zoomed-in at this point, to focus on the toy Painter. We will return to this tactic later when discussing creating locations.

Granny Smith Went Shopping

When I was young, we would frequently play the game *Granny Smith Went Shopping* on family occasions. I am sure you will be familiar with the game, though possibly under other names.

Player 1 starts by saying, "Granny Smith went shopping and she bought..." and they then add an item of their choosing. For example, "Granny Smith went shopping and she bought some tomatoes."

The second player would then recall the first item and add a second item of their own afterwards. So, they might say, "Granny Smith went shopping and she bought some tomatoes. And a ukulele." Often a player may try to add an item that would throw the other players.

It is then Player 3s turn and they could say, "Granny Smith went shopping and she bought some tomatoes. And a ukulele. And a pink balaclava..." And so on.

Simply put, every player has to recall what has gone before and then add their own item.

As a young child, we would have approximately a dozen people around a Christmas Table. Sometimes it would be less. At times, it could be up to 30. *Granny Smith Went Shopping* would then become an epic battle! However, over time, I was not allowed to participate in the game. That is for one simple reason – when you employ Memory Tools, it is easy to play indefinitely.

Try to remember the following 20 items off the top of your head, *without* using what you have learned so far:

Handbag

Turtle

Trumpet

Zucchini (Courgette)

Leather skirt

Milk

Bongos

Sunglasses

Pencil

Lamborghini

Button

Socks

Moisturiser

Elephant tusk

Muesli

Lemonade

Corset

Stretcher

Toenail Scissors

Broadsword

There are a couple of things to note about this list. Firstly, you will have noticed a nice mixture of normal and surreal items. Players will often try to throw-in something like, "Uncle Jim's burnt pancakes" in an attempt to derail their opponents. However, in reality, such items stand-out and are thus *more* memorable.

Secondly, you will see that players often try to flit all over the place and will jump from a diamond-encrusted Porsche to a ham sandwich. They try to make their item *completely* unrelated to the previous one. In practice, they often end up making an association obvious because they choose almost the complete opposite of the previous item (which therefore becomes easy to remember), or they choose something that appears unrelated, but is in fact a clear association (for example, in our list that would be jumping from toenail scissors to their more elaborate cousin - a Broadsword!).

Anyway, enough about the game. Here's how you win it and more importantly, why you might care.

You can play a game like this indefinitely by employing either of the two Linking methods we have discussed in this chapter:

Link item 1 to item 2. Then link item 2 to item 3...
Or:
Link item 1 to 2 and onto 3, naturally linking on to 4...

That is, you can link items together in pairs (as long as the pairs interlock with their neighbours, so to speak), or you can create one long continuous chain (or "story," as normal people might call it!).

At the moment, this might seem completely unrelated to the sort of challenges that face you as a therapist. However, before you write this off completely, I would invite you to return to our "Granny Smith" list using one of the linking methods we have mentioned. Speaking personally, if I was allowed to play, I would proceed as follows:

Granny Smith opens her handbag *and pulls out a* Turtle!
She then, in the middle of the supermarket, proceeds to play it like a trumpet. *As she does, a* courgette *shoots out of it's mouth!*
The courgette knocks over a woman in a leather skirt *and sends her carton of* milk *flying! The milk lands on a man playing the* bongos. *He is outraged, picks up his bongos and*

places them on his face like sunglasses, *before zooming-off in his* Lamborghini...

You will have noticed that most of the associations end with an exclamation point. That is, of course, completely intentional and fully endorses the SMASHIN' SCOPE concept we have written about previously.

The *Link Method* may seem too simple to be effective in the real world. Yet, it may interest you to know that Jonathan Hancock successfully used it (alongside one of the more basic Peg systems seen below[5]) to win the 1994 World Memory Championships!

In actual fact, before you have finished this book you will see that any effective memory tool is strengthened by skilful linking of items, no matter what additional techniques are employed.

---

5   The Peg system favoured by Jonathan Hancock, which he really stretched to show the capabilities of, was the Number-Shape system. See Jonathan Hancock, *Jonathan Hancock's Mindpower System,* Hodder & Stoughton, 1995,

Peg Systems

A peg system is a mnemonic technique for memorising lists. It works by pre-memorising a list of words that are easy to associate with the numbers they represent. Those words (which are almost always nouns) form the "pegs" that items to be remembered are then hung from.

Peg systems work by associating information you already know extremely well - for example, the letters of the alphabet, or the numbers 1 to 10 – with the new facts you want to remember. The more intricately the peg interacts with the item to be remembered, the more likely it is that it will be effective.

In one of the methods we will turn to shortly, a bee-hive is used to represent the number 5. (You can already see how simple this method is!) To remember that *Doctor* is the 5th word in a list you intend to recall, you would not merely think of the word *Doctor*, or even picture a doctor standing next to a bee-hive. Instead, you might see a doctor in a white coat, with a stethoscope, attempting to listen to the heart-beat of a bee-hive. Or you could see dozens of Bees flying around in little white coats!

You will see just how simple and yet remarkably effective Peg systems can be when we look at some examples of them in use. The three peg methods we will turn to now are:

- The Number Rhyme Method
- The Number Shape Method
- Alphabet Peg Systems

Number Rhyme

When I first learned about Memory systems, the Number-Rhyme system seemed especially attractive and intuitive to me. That may have been because of a children's nursery rhyme that was very familiar to me as a small boy:

This old man, he played one
He played knick-knack on my drum
With a knick-knack paddy whack
Give a dog a bone
This old man came rolling home

This old man, he played two
He played knick-knack on my shoe
With a knick-knack paddy whack
Give a dog a bone
This old man came rolling home

This old man, he played three

He played knick-knack on my tree
With a knick-knack paddy whack
Give a dog a bone
This old man came rolling home

This old man, he played four
He played knick-knack on my door
With a knick-knack paddy whack
Give a dog a bone
This old man came rolling home

This old man, he played five
He played knick-knack on my hive
With a knick-knack paddy whack
Give a dog a bone
This old man came rolling home

This old man, he played six
He played knick-knack on my stick
With a knick-knack paddy whack
Give a dog a bone
This old man came rolling home

This old man, he played seven
He played knick-knack up in heaven
With a knick-knack paddy whack

Give a dog a bone
This old man came rolling home

This old man, he played eight
He played knick-knack on my gate
With a knick-knack paddy whack
Give a dog a bone
This old man came rolling home

This old man, he played nine
He played knick-knack on my vine
With a knick-knack paddy whack
Give a dog a bone
This old man came rolling home

This old man, he played ten
He played knick-knack on my hen
With a knick-knack paddy whack
Give a dog a bone
This old man came rolling home

This Old Man has a complicated and diverse history in English history. Some have concluded that it is a racist song, but its roots seem to go way back before any of the words were used in a discriminatory manner.

Nevertheless, the point is that the method worked for me because *it meant something to me*, which you will know by now is an effective memory principle.

So, the gist of this Number-Rhyme Method has already been revealed, thanks to the song above. The main idea of the method is to translate numbers into more memorable images.

Here is how the method is often presented:

1 = Bun[6]

2 = Shoe

3 = Tree

4 = Door

5 = Hive

6 = Sticks[7]

7 = Heaven

8 = Gate[8]

9 = Vine[9]

10 = Hen / Pen

---

6 Bun or Gun are most often used, rather than Drum, as in the song.

7 A popular choice is Bricks instead of Sticks.

8 Be careful that you do not confuse Gate with Heaven (if picturing the pearly gates for the latter). My personal way round this is to picture Bill Gates.

9 Wine is an obvious alternative to Vine. I use both interchangeably, as they are related.

Hopefully, the benefit here seems obvious. Although we may more naturally think of the numbers 1-10, than their substitute words, you may find that it's easier to associate whatever is to be remembered to one of the words above than the numbers they represent.

Remembering Details from a Client's Life

For example, let's imagine that a client reveals a number of events in their life. For some reason, it may be useful to be able to remember them in order, along with their place in that order.

The events, or details to be remembered, may be something like:

Traumatic birth

Car crash

Fighting

Antidepressants

Fire Extinguisher

Divorce

Mini-Bus

Graduation

Camping

Public Speaking

To associate the items/images with their in-order associations, you might think of the following 10 images/scenes. (If you actually do imagine these scenes, rather than merely read my descriptions, you will see just how effective the method is!)

1. Someone painfully giving birth to a Chelsea Bun!

2. Two shoes violently crashing into each other

3. Your client trying to box with someone, but the Tree between them is getting in the way

4. A door deflating and then being pumped-up again

5. A Bee-Hive on fire, being extinguished by your client

6. A Wedding Officiant at the front of a church snapping sticks in half and declaring them divorced

7. A Bus driving a group of elderly passengers to

Heaven

8. Bill Gates giving the Graduation speech at your College

9. Someone trying to set-up their camp, but a growing vine keeps poking through the tent

10. A hen giving a TED Talk!

It should be fairly obvious how this works. When you later need to recall the list, you need only think through the numbers 1-10 and think of your key-words. So, you might need to recall the 5th item and think of a Bee-hive. You will then easily remember the image of a Bee-hive in flames, being extinguished by your client.

Try it out for yourself and you may be surprised how many items from the list – and therefore events from your client's life – you can now remember.

Extending the System

The Number-Rhyme system can easily be extended to include the numbers 11-20, if so desired. The following suggested rhymes may not be as intuitive, but they demonstrate that you can recall up to 20 items with this method:

11. Leaven (bread)

12. Elf, shelf

13. Flirting, thirsting (Robinson Crusoe dying of thirst)

14. Courting (Juliet courting, or a High Court Judge)

15. Fitting, lifting (Weight-lifter)

16. Sistine (chapel), shifting, sitting

17. Javelin, deafening

18. Aching, aiding, waiting (Waiter or... "a king"!)

19. Knighting

20. Plenty (I simply use an image of a popular brand of Kitchen Roll in the UK.)

To make these truly memorable, I convert them into nouns/objects. You would then associate items with the numbered peg words, precisely as you did with the numbers 1-10.

Number Shape

The Number-Shape peg system is similar to the Number-Rhyme system, but instead of using words that rhyme with the numbers, you use the shape of the number as the peg. You guessed that though, right?

So, for example, the number 1 might be represented by an image of a candle, because 1 looks somewhat like a candle.

Then, to associate an item with a number, you simply connect it to the image that resembles the shape of the number. For example, to associate a word such as "pineapple" to position number two in the list, you would associate a swan (the number 2) with a pineapple (the item to be remembered).

You might imagine a swan painfully bouncing a prickly pineapple up and down on its beak. Then, when you think of the second item in the list, it reminds you of the swan, which makes you recall the image and thus the word, "pineapple."

Some popular number shape images include:

0 = ball, egg, doughnut, ring

1 = candle, stick, spear, pole

2 = swan, clothes hanger

3 = butterfly, handcuffs, heart,

4 = flag, sail-boat, chair

5 = hook, snake, seahorse

6 = elephant's trunk, golf club, cherry, spoon

7 = boomerang, axe, scythe, kite, diving board

8 = snowman, hourglass

9 = balloon on a string, boxer's glove

10 = Cricket bat and ball, knife and plate

Using these peg words to memorise data works exactly as it did with the number-rhyme method. To demonstrate that, let us remember the top 10 best-selling books of all time (according to some lists. No need to quibble here!).

1. Don Quixote

2. A Tale of Two Cities

3. The Lord of the Rings

4. The Little Prince

5. Harry Potter and the Philosopher's Stone

6. And Then There Were None

7. The Hobbit

8. Alice's Adventures in Wonderland

9. The Lion, The Witch, and the Wardrobe

10. She: A History of Adventure

To memorise this list, we will simply pick an image to represent each title and then connect that image to our number-shape image. My associations are offered below, yet, as always, it is more effective if you choose your own.

1. This is the first item, so I will be using the image of a candle. So, I picture a candle being used to set fire to a

Piñata in the shape of a donkey, releasing hundreds of oaty snacks. Of course, a donkey makes me think of Don Quixote!

You might prefer to choose an image from one of the Godfather films, with Don Corleone, or a friend of yours named Donald.

2. Our second item needs to be connected to the image of a swan, representing the number 2. I picture a swan, located in Derby cathedral (Derby being a city in the UK that I happen to know well), flicking through a book that turns out to be simply a series of maps of various cities. This makes me think of 'A Tale of Two Cities.'

3. Some people use a butterfly for the number 3 in a number-shape system. However, I prefer to have only one flying creature (the swan). So, the number 3 becomes a heart, which then is represented by a friend of mine who is a Cardiologist. I picture him performing heart surgery on someone and pulling out a precious ring, which naturally makes me think of 'Lord of the Rings.'

4. Number 4 is represented for me by a yacht (with its sail). So, I see a miniature Prince Charles trying to steer a

boat into Buckingham Palace. Thus, when I think of the 4th item, I immediately know it is *The Little Prince*.

5. For me, number 5 is a seahorse. It's possibly a controversial choice, but you cannot deny that they are cute! However, you may want to consider if a seahorse could be confused with a yacht (my number 4), as they are both at sea.

I simply picture Daniel Radcliffe (as Harry Potter) riding a seahorse, whilst playing Quidditch. He is desperately trying not to drop a stone that he is holding. When I think of this scene, I instantly recall that the 5th item in my list is *Harry Potter and the Philosopher's Stone*.

6. This book may be troublesome if you do not know it. Personally, I think of Agatha Christie on a Golf Course (a golf club being my number 6), trying to hit a Nun (i.e. 'none') across the green! That's my way of remembering that the 6th book is *And Then There Were None*, by Agatha Christie.

7. My number 7 is a diving board. I simply picture Bilbo Baggins ('The Hobbit') nervously attempting to dive into a pile of goblins!

8. Naturally, my number 8 is a snowman. There are all sorts of possibilities here. I would choose to picture a snowman attempting to crawl down a rabbit-hole, to remind me that the 8th book in our list is *Alice in Wonderland*.

9. For my 9th item, which is *The Lion, the Witch and the Wardrobe*, I picture a Lion in a hot-air balloon, where the basket is actually made out of a wardrobe. (Number 9 for me is a balloon on a string, which normally becomes a hot-air balloon in most of my images!)

10. Number 10, for me, is a cricket bat and ball. I see She-ra (from the He-man cartoons) hitting my history teacher – who is dressed like Indiana Jones - across the field. That helps me easily recall that the 10th book is *She: A History of Adventure*.

I appreciate that such a series of images may seem ridiculous, unwieldy and ineffective. However, if you imagined them with me, how many of the items can you now recall?

Extending the System

It is actually possible to use a number-shape method to convert all of the numbers from 00 to 99 into images. In some ways, this makes it more like the system we will encounter in the chapter on Remembering Numbers. However, for now, it is encouraging to see how such a simple system can be used to represent all of the numbers up to 99.

Some of the following associations are less about the shape and more about the natural association. (For example, many Westerners would naturally think of Santa Claus for the number 25.) Others might include flipping numbers on their side, or placing one of the digits upside down. On the whole, this sort of extension moves us beyond a simple peg system. Yet, it is included here merely to demonstrate the deceptive power of such a simple system.

00 = Binoculars | Bongo drums | headphones

01 = Shield & Spear

02 = Hoover

03 = Rabbit

04 = Chopping board & Knife

05 = Lantern Torch With a Handle

06 = Golf Ball & Golf Club

07 = Megaphone | Grenade

08 = Pool Ball - Black Ball with 8 on it

09 = Tennis Ball & Racket

10 = Fat Man

11 = Drum Sticks

12 = Needle & Thread | Playground Slides

13 = Pregnant woman

14 = A man sitting cross-legged | Heart | Red Rose (Associated, Valentine's Day)

15 = Someone pushing a Wheelchair

16 = Man smoking Pipe | Man pulling a trolley

17 = Harp | Woodpecker

18 = Broom & Snowman

19 = Elephant

20 = Snail

21 = Dollar sign

22 = Pair of High heel Shoes

23 = Swan - Neck-body-tail

24 = Alarm Clock (Associated, i.e. 24 hours)

25 = Santa's sleigh (Associated, i.e. Dec. 25th)

26 = Watering can

27 = Trowel

28 = Crocodile

29 = Gondola and man

30 = Jelly Fish

31 = Lips smoking cigarette | Bow & Arrow

32 = Shark in wavy sea

33 = Seagull

34 = Goat with Horns

35 = Crane Hook

36 = Lips smoking pipe

37 = Rocket

38 = Beetle Car

39 = Lips blowing a Party Whistle

40 = Concrete Mixer Truck

41 = Man Jet Skiing

42 = Horse Head and Neck curve

43 = Fish

44 = Suspension bridge

45 = Kite & string

46 = SeaHorse

47 = Chihuahua

48 = Pick up Van (8 tilted down as the wheels)

49 = Mice eating a block of cheese

50 = Tractor

51 = Pipe Wrench

52 = Cards - Dealing playing cards (Associated)

53 = Bra

54 = Snake and his head

55 = Wheelbarrow

56 = Forklift

57 = Blacksmith Anvil

58 = Scooter (8 tilted down as wheels)

59 = Bull fight - Bull head-butting

60 = Monkeys Tail and Body - Monkey eating a Banana

61 = Fishing Tackle

62 = Cat

63 = Bee

64 = Laptop, 64 bit - (Associated)

65 = Muscle Arm & Bicep

66 = Two Cherries with a leaf

67 = Punch Machine

68 = Pram

69 = Yin Yang

70 = Straw in a cocktail glass

71 = Fire Extinguisher

72 = Water pump

73 = Camel

74 = Semi Automatic Handgun

75 = Exercise Bike

76 = Saxophone

77 = Two men rowing a boat | two bent legs

78 = Shopping cart (8 tilted down as wheels)

79 = Axe and Farmer

80 = Baby Dummy

81 = Violin and bow

82 = Woman swinging her hair

83 = Mermaid - Slapping her tail

84 = Bride and Groom (arm) - Bride holding arm with the broom and walking

85 = Girl on a Unicycle

86 = Girl blowing a Whistle

87 = Frog Eyes & Mouth

88 = Weights

89 = Snorkel

90 = Ninja Turtle

91 = Space suit

92 = Lion

93 = Butterfly

94 = Chef & Knife

95 = Squirrel

96 = Key & Padlock

97 = Old Man & his walking stick

98 = Biker with helmet

99 = Scissors | Mushrooms | Balloons

My suggestion, if you wanted to extend the Number-Shape system from 00 to 99 in this way, would be ensure you come up with your own images as far as possible. It is essential that you reach the point where you do not have to think too hard of the image that the number represents. In some ways, that would defeat the whole point of the system and just give you something else you have to try to remember.

Instead, put the effort in to devise a system that – perhaps with some initial work on your part – gives you an immediate association between the number and its representative shape-image.

Alphabet Peg Systems

It is not clear who originally devised the idea of using the Alphabet as a Peg system. However, it is perhaps so obvious that any number of people could claim that credit.

We will start by looking at the easiest and most natural way to create a Peg list from the letters of the Alphabet. Then we will explore some additional methods and finally look at Advanced applications.

Alphabet System

The most natural way for many of us to employ an alphabet system might be to think of the words that were used for us to learn the letters in the first place. This will vary from culture to culture, but might look something like:

A = Apple

B = Banana

C = Cat

D = Dog

E = Egg

F = Fire Engine

G = Goat

H = Hen

I = Igloo

K = Kite

L = Lemon

M = Moon

N = Nail

O = Owl

P = Pig

Q = Queen

R = Rainbow

S = Sun

T = Teacher

U = Umbrella

V = Van

W = Water

X = X-Ray

Y = Yacht

Z = Zoo

The point with such a list is that it should be automatic. The words you choose should be iconic. It should not be a case of thinking, "Okay, what does the letter D make me think of?" Instead, the process needs to be "D is Dog." So if you do not have words that are naturally brought to mind when you think of the letter, the methods below may be preferable to you.

I am confident that you do not need any further explanation regarding how to use an Alphabet Peg Method. You simply use the peg words to recall the items to be remembered, as you did with the Number-Rhyme and Number-Shape systems. However, there are some alternative ways that you may want to compile your list.

Phonetic Alphabet

To create a peg-list from the letters of the Alphabet, you can simply use the *sound* of each letter to remind you of a peg-word. Examples might include:

A = Ace

B = Bee

C = Sea

D = Deed

E = Eels

F = Effigy

G = Jeep

H = Aches

I = Eye

J = Jay (bird)

K = Cake

L = Elbow

M = Ember

N = Entrance / Hen

O = Oboe

P = Peach

Q = Queue

R = Ark

S = Eskimo

T = Tea

U = Ukulele

V = Vehicle

W = W.C. (Toilet)

X = X-ray

Y = Wife / Wifi

Z = Zebra

You will most likely have grasped by now that it is usually easier to use nouns for your peg-words, as they more naturally translate into images. So, looking at the above words, I would probably picture a famous Poker Player I know for *Ace*. *Sea* might become a Cruise Liner, or a Lighthouse. *Deed* might become Adam Sandler, from the film Mr. Deeds. And so on...

You will see that the important thing is not to be overly loyal to the rules of the alphabet. The vital thing is to use the word that the letter most naturally makes you think of. Here are some ideas that might assist with compiling your own list:

1. Use the sound of the letter, not words that begin with that letter

For example, C made us think of the word Sea. So, we stick with that. This is because it takes longer to pause and think of words that begin with that letter. The sound of the letter is obvious the second we hear it, so we use that.

2. Use words that are first in the alphabet

This one is presumably quite obvious. If D did not give you any words that begin with a "Dee" sound, then you might then think of words beginning with D. The key then is to think of the first word in the alphabet, which you can easily recall later. In this case, we would look at words beginning with "Da" and opt for "Dad."

3. If no word occurs to you, use abbreviations

W is a good example here. In reality, I would probably think of George W. Bush. However, let's presume that we could not think of a word beginning with the sound "Dub" and no other association leapt out at us. It is then worth thinking of initials, possibly even before you spell words out (as we did with Dad above). This is because you are still using the sound of the word.

For example, again employing the letter W, *W.C.* probably comes up more quickly than *Wax*, when we hear the letter as we are simply following the sound. However, your mileage may vary on this point.

Alphabet Shape

The previous means of using the alphabet resembled

the Number-Rhyme system in that it was sound-based. This method, as the name implies, is shape-based.

Here are the kinds of images that the shape of the letters makes me think of:

A = Geometric compass

B = Brassiere

C = Banana

D = Crescent moon

E = Comb

F = Scythe

G = Sickle

H = Chimney pot

I = Candle

J = Hockey stick

K = Picnic table (on its side)

L = L-square

M = Fedora

N = Crank handle

O = Doughnut

P = Sword with hilt

Q = Penny-farthing Bicycle

R = Pincers

S = Snake

T = Sledgehammer

U = Horseshoe

V = Hand fan

W = Badminton birdie

X = Diabolo

Y = Cocktail glass

Z = Folding ruler

If those images do not work for you, what about:

A = Easel

B = Sunglasses

C = Moon

D = Pregnant Woman

E = Fork

F = Toothbrush

G = Ear

H = Step Ladder

I = Needle

J = Umbrella

K – Acrobat (doing the splits)

L - A sniper + gun

M - Spider

N - Compass [North]

O - Bracelet | Tyre

P - Flag on a pole

Q – Magnifying Glass | Ring

R - Ribbon Badge

S - Superman

T - T-Ruler

U - Cup

V - Necklace | Ice-Cream Cone

W - Vampire Teeth

X – Plasters | Map (X marks the spot!)

Y - Slingshot | Funnel

Z - Escalator

Topical Alphabet

One of the activities that my children and I enjoy is walking. Well, it might be more accurate to say that *I* enjoy walking and I take them with me! Before they had resigned themselves to this fate, they would occasionally complain that they were bored on a walk. A game that I used on such occasions was the Alphabet Game. The rules are fairly obvious.

We would pick a topic and then take turns naming something related to that topic, according to consecutive letters of the alphabet. So, if the topic was Food, the game may proceed as follows:

A = Apple

B = Banana

C = Carrot

D = Doughnut

E = Eggs

F = Fish

G = Grapes

H = Halloumi

I = Ice-cream

J = Jelly

K = Kiwi

L = Lemon

M = Mango

N = Nachos

O = Onions

P = Peas

Q = Quinoa

R = Rice

S = Salami

T = Tomatoes

U = Upside-down Pineapple Cake

V = Veal

W = Watermelon

X = Xmas Pudding(!)

Z = Zucchini

There are practically an infinite number of topics you could come up with: games, boys names, cars, TV shows, candy bars and so on. This gives you countless alphabet lists you could later call upon.

The important thing here is that the letter makes you think of that word first every time. You do not want to have to come up with a dozen words for every letter, whilst hunting for your peg. Also, as you can see, the letter X can be a real struggle!

An additional issue with topical alphabets is ensuring that the images that your peg-words conjure up are distinct enough to be remembered. For example, are Kiwi, Lemon and Mango going to be too similar in the images they bring to mind? One way round this is to use the word as a trigger to think of something else. So, for me, the word *Kiwi* makes me think of the New Zealand Rugby team. *Mango* makes me think of an Indian Restaurant I enjoy visiting, because they serve the most delicious Mango Lassis. And Lemon makes me think of, well,

Lemons! However, you might prefer to think of someone selling lemonade on the side of the street.

Alphabet as Location

This use of the Alphabet really belongs in the next chapter. However, we will include it here and then refer back to it at a later point.

You can use the letters of the Alphabet, not just to think of specific items, but to refer to locations. We will unpack the benefits of this later, but for now you might think of:

A = Ark

B = Beach

C = Corner shop

D = Dungeon

E = Elevator

F = Fire Station

G = Goal (on Football pitch)

H = Hospital

I = Eiffel Tower

J = Jail

K = Kwik-Fit (chain of garages in the UK)

L = London Tower

M = Mountain (or Climbing wall)

N = Niagara Falls

O = Oxford University

P = Pyramind

Q = Quayside

R = Red Sea

S = Sea-World Centre

T = Taj Mahal

U = Underground Station

V = Victoria & Albert Museum

W = Waterloo

X = Exeter

Y = York Minster

Z = Zoo

It will not surprise you here to know that the key is to come up with memorable and distinct locations *that work for you*. For example, the town of Exeter is too vague to be reliable. However, as the journey there was the first train trip I ever went on as a child, it has special memories for me. So, I naturally do not simply think of the town, but a certain point I recall from that trip.

A mountain may be too vague if you have never

climbed one, or seen one up close. However, there is no reason it cannot make you think of a Climbing Wall at your local Gym. Kwik-fit works for me as I can think of the garage where I take my car. You may prefer to think of your local K-Mart, or even the city of Kolkata, India.

Anyway, what is all of this talk of locations about? I am glad you asked. Sit back, belt up and prepare to take things to the next level!

Location, Location, Location!

One of the most significant discoveries of recent years, for memory enthusiasts, has actually been a *re*-discovery. That is the importance and effectiveness of using locations as a memory tool. The device goes by many names – Roman Room, Memory Palace, the Journey Method – yet the most accurate term is probably simply the *method of Loci*.[10]

The method of loci is a means of memorising information by placing each item to be remembered at a point on a specific location, or even along an imaginary journey. (*Loci* is the plural of the Latin word, *locus*, meaning place or location.)

The information can then be recalled in a specific order by simply retracing the same route through the journey. As such, the method relies upon the use of visualization and spatial memory to quickly and efficiently memorise,

---

10 There are actually some minor differences between the methods referred to by these descriptions. However, that need not concern us here.

organise and recall information.

This method is a mnemonic device adopted in ancient Roman and Greek rhetorical texts by writers such as Cicero and Quintilian. In fact, the earliest known explicit description of the method of loci is in the *Rhetorica ad Herennium*, written sometime around 90 BCE.

Roman legend attributed the method to the Greek poet, Simonides of Ceos, who discovered the technique while identifying bodies in the wreckage of a collapsed building that he had been sitting in just moments before. The story is that Simonides stepped-out of a room seconds before it collapsed. In order to identify the bodies, the poet simply visualised who was located where and thus recalled the information.

Yet, whilst historical records of the technique only go back to Simonides in the 6th Century BCE, the method of loci goes far back into prehistory. Lynne Kelly has written extensively on the use of this technique in oral (i.e. pre-literal) cultures. Examples include mnemonic techniques that involve spacial relationship such as song lyrics and Memory Boards (like Lukasas) and perhaps even physical structures, such as Stonehenge![11]

---

11 See Lynne Kelly, *The Memory Code: The Traditional Aboriginal Memory Technique that Unlocks the Secrets of Stonehenge, Easter Island and Ancient Monuments the World Over*. Atlantic Books, 2017.

Some fictional characters have been known to employ this method, including Hannibal Lecter and Sherlock Holmes. (However, the latter uses the term *Mind Palace* and refers to an expanded use of Memory Palaces for more than mere recall.)

Creating a Memory Journey

To experience the power of the method of Loci, let's create a mental journey along a well-known route, for example, through your house. For the purposes of this example, we are going to devise a 16-stage journey.

The first 16 loci, or locations, of the journey might be:

1. Bedroom - Window

2. Bedroom – on the bed

3. Bathroom

4. Hallway

5. Second Bedroom with the large wardrobe

6. Top of stairs

7. Bottom of Stairs

8. Living room – sofa

9. Living room - bookcase

10.   Living room – television

11.   Dining room

12.   Kitchen

13.   Front door (from the inside)

14.   Front porch

15.   Front Garden

16.   Driveway

Obviously, this journey will not mean the same to you that it does to me. This relates back to our earliest principle of Association. You have to be able to identify something in order to associate with and to it. So it is always more effective to come up with your own links, locations and associations.

To really demonstrate the effectiveness of this method, you will benefit from devising your own journeys. Nevertheless, for the purposes of this example, I will proceed with this journey.

These 16 locations will function as our first "memory palace." Incidentally, we will always travel through the palace or journey in the same order. That is one of the differences between this and a simple Roman Room, but I said I was not going to get into that!

Memorise the Items

This really is about as simple as it gets! In order to utilise our journey, we need only take a list of 16 items that we want to memorize, then imagine each item in one locus, or location, of our memory palace.

It helps if you do not merely place the item at the location, but have the two (that is, the item and the location) interact with each other in some way. So, for full effectiveness, do not merely have The Incredible Hulk standing in front of the TV in your lounge. Instead, have him smashing the television, or picking it up and throwing it across the room.

For example, you could try memorizing the following list. This is the order that certain therapeutic methodologies were developed:

- Mesmerism

- Psychoanalysis

- Alfred Adler's Individual Psychology

- Carl Jung Analytical Psychology

- Rogers Client-Centred Therapy

- Gestalt Therapy

- Behavioural therapy (B. F. Skinner)

- Humanistic psychology (E.g. Maslow)

- Rational Emotive Behaviour Therapy

- Logotherapy.

- Reality Therapy

- CBT

- Primal therapy

- SFBT

- ACT

- Narrative Therapy

To make such a list memorable, we would convert each item into a key image. For example, mesmerism might become a swinging watch, or a famous hypnotist you know and can easily picture or think of. Behavioural Therapy might be pictured as a drooling dog and so on.

Next, using the sample journey above, you would place a swinging watch in the first locus of the memory palace, which is in your bedroom, in front of the window. You might want to exaggerate things, by having a suitably "hypnotic" individual swing his watch so vigorously that it smashes the window.

Then, place the second item in the list at the second location of the memory palace and so on. Here is how I would approach this particular example:

1. In the bedroom, in front of the Window, Richard Nongard is swinging a watch so energetically that it smashes the window.

2. On the bed, my own mother is frantically trying to get under the bed covers, wearing my pyjamas, whilst recounting experiences from her childhood. It's Freud – enough said!

3. I open the door to the bathroom to find it teeming in snakes (adders remind me of Alfred Adler)

4. I quickly leave and enter the Hallway, where I see my cousin Carl as a child, throwing a tantrum (as he was

prone to do when he was younger!). "Carl" and "young" remind me of Carl Jung.

5. When I move into the second Bedroom, Roger Rabbit is digging up the floorboards in front of the wardrobe, looking for carrots!

6. At the top of stairs, an animated Pearl necklace (signifying Fritz Perlz) is talking to an empty chair (to remind me of Gestalt Therapy).

7. When I reach the bottom of the Stairs, I find a dog drooling on the bottom step, with a heavy bell tied to its collar.

8. In the Living room, on the sofa, I find Abraham Lincoln (which makes me think of Abraham Maslow) building a pyramid (to represent Maslow's hierarchy of need).

9. Turning to look at the bookcase, I see my friend Ellis (Albert Ellis) weeping (Emotional) as he reads some of my books. He is crying so much (a ridiculously exaggerated amount) that his tears are damaging the pages, much to

my annoyance!

10. In front of the television, Naomi Klein (author of the excellent book, '*No Logo*') is ironically sticking a bunch of logos and stickers onto the television, which is playing the movie, *Frankenstein* (Victor Frankl was the developer of Logotherapy).

11. In the dining room, my cousin William is about to vomit after eating an exceptionally enormous bowl of glacé cherries (William Glasser came up with Reality Therapy).

12. Beck, a favourite musician of mine, is moonwalking across the kitchen, whilst singing "CBT"! This one is personal, as CBT always makes me think of the song ABC by The Jackson 5!

13. As I reach the front door, I see Dudley Moore playing his character from the movie *Arthur*, screaming out of the letterbox. (Arthur Janov developed the rather dubious Primal Therapy.)

14. As I open the front door and step onto the porch, I

see Steve de Shazer (developer of SFBT) with a giant magnifying glass, crawling around on his hands and knees looking for clues/solutions. Obviously, this one works for me because I know what Steve de Shazer looks like. You could substitute him for someone you know named Steve, or Shaz!

15. On my front lawn, there are inexplicably numerous bales of hay. Naturally, these remind me of Steve Hayes, developer of Acceptance and Commitment Therapy (ACT).

16. I go to unlock my car, on the driveway, to find that it has been replaced by an unrealistically large Arm-chair. Sat in the chair is Tom Hardy (perhaps dressed as his character *Bane*, from *The Dark Knight Rises*). This reminds me of the unusual sight of Tom Hardly reading a bedtime story to our nation's children on the BBC show *CBeebies Bedtime Stories*. That makes me think of Narrative Therapy. Of course, you could have just had a ridiculously large book, perhaps laying on a stereotypical therapist's couch!

Recall the Items

To recall the items, all you need to do now is mentally retrace your route through the journey and you should be able to retrieve the data.

Of course, if you have used my location points *and* my images, then that list may not be as memorable to you as it is to me. Nevertheless, I am still fairly confident that you will already be able to see how effective this technique is and perhaps recall more than you expected.

If you want to store the memorised information for a longer period of time, use repetition and go through the memory palace a few times per day until it sticks.

After you have seen how easy it can be to memorise 16 items and can recite them forwards and backwards in order, try expanding your memory palace to 26 locations and see if you can do the same with 26 items. Then 52. Then 100!

It may seem that the method of Loci merely provides us with another series of peg words, much as we saw with the *Alphabet as Locations* method. Whilst there is an element of truth to this insight, there is more to the method than this.

Journeys combine all of the memory principles we have

so far encountered. Effectively, a journey is a story - a link. Also, it organises data in a logical progression. Finally, it involves association as you convert whatever is to be remembered into a memorable image and then enmesh it somehow with the location. In that sense, the method of Loci is both a peg system and a link method. No wonder it is so effective, highly regarded and historically utilised.

This could be why the method of Loci has been employed by so many cultures – often independent of each other – throughout human history. It seems that this may simply be how the human memory works. Have you ever tried to recall a sentence from a book you were reading and been surprised to find that you could even picture where in the page it was written? Or maybe you recognise someone and your immediate thought is *"where do I know them from?"*

Creating Journeys

I know, from painful personal experience, how difficult it can be (or seem to be) to devise enough memory journeys to be practically useful. Here are a few ideas to consider, each one a useful means of devising journeys:

Childhood homes

This is perhaps the most common choice, for good reason. Many of us will have spent years in a family home, in our formative years. I will add one caveat at this point, that you are free to experiment with and then take on board or reject.

My recommendation is not to use your current home, unless you have to. In my own personal experience, the home you now live in is best kept for *ad hoc* items that you need to remember in impromptu situations. As such, it may not be best for recalling long-term information.

Schools

Schools, Colleges, Universities, Libraries and Museums all make extremely useful memory palaces. You may want to allocate them to specific uses – for example, the National History Museum in London might be best served to recall historical dates, whilst your High School may be useful to remember the periodic table. However, any such building that you know thoroughly will serve you well.

Familiar routes

Any journey that you have done time and time again is useful. I prefer to walk, rather than drive, so a number of my journeys are routes I have walked to various places of employment, romantic walks I have taken, family days out and so on.

TV Studios

I will admit it, I am a geek. Thus, one of the first journeys I developed was around the set of *The Big Bang Theory*. This worked for me because I knew the show very very well. (Too well?) If you search online, you should be able to find floor plans for shows such as *Seinfeld*, *Friends*, *How I Met Your Mother*, *The Simpsons* and so on.

Film scenes

Are there any movies that you know really well? One of mine is *Good Will Hunting*. So, it is no problem for me to go through the film and select 26 key scenes in different locations. You might want to try it with films you know well.

Book plots

This is exactly the same idea as the film scenes above. Take any fictional book you know well – *Jane Eyre*, *Girl on the Train*, *The Curious Incident of the Dog in the Night Time*, etc. - and select a number of key plot points. Ensure they have their own distinct location and employ these to devise a journey.

Here is a quick example, using key points from Alice in Wonderland:

1. Dreaming in the tree
2. Following the rabbit
3. Falling down the hole
4. The big room
5. Inside a bottle
6. Running around the fire
7. With Tweedledum and Tweedledee
8. Carpenter's story
9. The rabbit's house garden
10. Rabbit's house entrance
11. Rabbit's room
12. Flowers
13. Hookah smoking caterpillar
14. Cheshire cat
15. Mad tea party
16. Lost and mourning with weird animals
17. Labyrinth
18. Painting roses
19. The queen's croquet
20. The trial

Album tracks

This will only work with some albums. I confess that I am a bit out of touch when it comes to contemporary music. However, if there are any albums that you are very familiar with – I personally think of *Pet Sounds*, *Thriller*, *Astral Weeks*, *Dark Side of the Moon* and suchlike – choose a different location to represent each track and use the album as a journey.

Computer Games

I'm exposing my geek side again, aren't I? Nevertheless, this can work for games as varied as *Jet Set Willy* and *Fortnite*. In fact, for many games, the whole idea is built around a journey.

Whilst we are on the subject, there are games where the very purpose is to construct your own world. So, why not use these to build memory palaces or create journeys?

Anything you know well!

Are you a history buff? Perhaps you can use a famous battle as a sort of journey, or choose locations for various points in a time-line you are familiar with. Or perhaps you can remember a place of employment? The only real limitation here is your own imagination.

Additional Tips

Some pointers you may want to consider in designing your own journeys include:

- Start inside, perhaps with a set number of loci

For some reason, this is how most of my journeys have developed over time. It really is quite useful because if you pay attention, any one room can easily provide you with an average of 4-6 loci. In fact, I would expect to find 8-10 locations in any one room.

- Then move outside

After I have started my journey in e.g. my house, I then move outside and have far more reference points to use. Lampposts, Garages, Bus-stops, post boxes, shops, lawns, telephone boxes, litter bins, the spot where I always pass the old lady walking her dog, and on and on...

Some people recommend keeping your loci an equal distance apart. This can be helpful, as your memory will anticipate when the next item to be remembered can be found. However, I have not found it to be essential.

The key is to use distinct points. I may have more than one bus-stop on a journey, but one is on the left side of a quiet road and is in perfect condition. The other is on the right side of a busy road and has a warped roof (which I often utilise in some way).

- Fixed points with familiar items (e.g. bridge)

The one downside that I can think of for journeys – aside from having to prepare them in advance – is that (unlike the number-rhyme system) you may struggle to instantly locate an item at a specific point. For example, you may have easily memorised the 16 therapeutic developments above, but can you recall what the 11th item was? (Hint: My cousin William is eating cherries!)

One way round this is to have familiar items at specific points. For example, each 10th item may be a bridge. Every 5th item could be bright red and so on.

- You can zoom in, either with specific items, or by giving clues, e.g. magnifying glass, colour red, etc.

Do you remember us zooming-in on the train track? Sure you do! A kitten jumped on a child's toy train, where a (toy) painter was painting an ocean on the outside of the Station. Remember? The ocean became a rainbow?

Zooming-in is an incredibly useful technique for developing more loci. The only problem is that during recall it would be easy to rush past a toy train, not realising that you were supposed to zoom-in for 10 more location points! One way round this is to have clues at each location where you are required to zoom-in. An obvious choice would be a magnifying-glass, or binoculars. Alternatively, you could even simply rely on particular colours to highlight to you that there is a need to pause and pay special attention to the finer details. Or, ensure that you always zoom-in on certain items. For example, if there is ever a sink in one of my journeys it is almost always zoomed-in on to provide as many loci as you might expect from a swimming pool!

- Use Certain journeys for specific subjects, e.g. art museum for paintings

We have already alluded to this. Many people find that it makes sense to use e.g. libraries for lists of authors, art museums for famous paintings, school buildings for subjects such as Maths, Science and English, and so on.

- Use Journeys of different lengths

Of course, it is up to you to decide how many journeys you need, of whatever length. However, I find it useful to have a number of journeys of the following four lengths:

- 10 stages

- 26 stages (25 loci might be more intuitive, yet 26 is useful for memorising packs of cards)

- 52 stages (why stick to 50, when you can have 52?!)
- 100 stages

And Finally...

Now here is something interesting. (Though take this with a pinch of salt, as I am neither a linguist nor a historian!) It appears that our term "topic" derives from the days of Greek oratory. In particular, from memory devices used by Greek orators.

The word "topic" comes from the Greek word, *topos* meaning *place*. It is believed that the word was chosen because Orators would store each subject they had to speak on at various *topos* along a route.

This may also explain a common rhetorical phrase, "In the first place," which seems to refer to the first stage in a journey, to remind someone of the first thing they wished to say.

Feel free to share that fascinating fact with anyone who asks how Memory Tools can be useful!

Remembering Numbers

The world of competitive memory changed when Dominic O'Brien appeared on the scene. Dominic had been inspired by watching someone memorise a deck of cards on the TV show *Record Breakers* in 1987.[12] He then went ahead and devised his own means of repeating that stunt.

Dominic made two massive contributions to Memory Sports: the rediscovery of the importance of Location and his own method of converting numbers into letters. We have already spoken at length on the *Method of Loci*. Dominic inspired thousands of memory enthusiasts by opening the door to the Roman Room and encouraging people to go outside. He called it the Journey Method, but it is simply Loci unleashed. This was perhaps his most useful contribution.

However, his simplest innovation was finding a simple and memorable way of converting numbers into letters (and therefore into words, which are more easily

____

12 Cf. Dominic O'Brien, *How to Develop a Perfect Memory*, p. 149.

remembered). Dominic suggested the following conversions:

$$0 = O$$
$$1 = A$$
$$2 = B$$
$$3 = C$$
$$4 = D$$
$$5 = E$$
$$6 = S$$
$$7 = G$$
$$8 = H$$
$$9 = N$$

This is self-explanatory, though it is worth highlighting that 6 and 9 do not follow the usual alphabetical order of the others. Dominic surmised that people may more naturally (and swiftly) translate those letters into their phonetic beginnings. I think he made the right choice.[13]

---

13 The only letter that I think sometimes throws beginners is 7. I know one competitor who used V instead of G, as that was a letter that stood out for him for that number (and of course S is taken by 6!). However, they soon found that they could not come up with as many words beginning with V as they needed to. Another option would be to use F for 6 and then you are free to use S for 7. I think this is simply a question of which conversion takes place the most intuitively for you.

Now, here is where it gets interesting. To expand that system to include 100 numbers, you obviously simply put two letters side by side. So, 84 is HD and 23 is BC.

That's simple enough, right? The only issue is that such two-letter combinations are not easily converted into words. Well, here is where many people feel that Dominic really added a simple yet highly significant insight, derived from the fact that his early memory attempts were focused on Playing Cards. Dominic does not suggest using HD to make up words (e.g. HiD or HuDdle, etc.), but as initials for <u>characters</u>. Dominic's insight was that many of us find people much easier to remember than abstract words or even non-living nouns.

So, this means that 84 might become HD, which in my list is Helen Daniels (an early character in the Soap Opera *Neighbours*). I do not personally always use the number-letter conversion suggested by Dominic. That is because some numbers simply leap out at you and it would be counter-productive to force a different association to the one your mind comes up with. An example of this for me is the number 4. In Dominic's system, 04 converts to the letters O and D. However, I do not use that as initials, because OD makes me think of a drug-user (over-dose). Another irregular conversion is 02 (OB), which becomes

Obi-Wan Kenobe from the *Star Wars* films.

However, sometimes you can jump a stage and won't even need to convert the number to letters. We saw this back with the first list of numbers we looked at where 31 conjured up the memorable image of a fire-fighter for me. Similarly, 10 made me think of 10 Downing Street. So, I simply think of Tony Blair, who used to live there.

Who is in *Your* List?

So, here is where I get *you* to do some work. I would encourage you to grab pen and paper, or turn-on your computer and write-up your own list of characters from 00 (OO) to 99 (NN).

*** Here is an important bit: Your characters will be more memorable if they have a distinct action that you automatically associate with them. We will also use this to extend the list further later on. ***

I am aware that it may feel as if we are stepping into more complicated territory here. To be honest, if you have no need to memorise numbers, or are happy converting 3 to a Tree, or 7 into a kite, you can probably skip most of this chapter. However, I would urge you to continue. I am going to ask you to exert what amounts to minimal effort for some fairly exceptional returns. Trust me, I've been there and I remain grateful to this day that I put in the effort to learn this. There is honestly not a single day that goes by without me using my list!

Get those brain-cells working and come up with your own list of 100 people, with distinct actions. Here is an example list - of People and their Actions – that you might want to consider for inspiration:

00 = OO = Ozzy Osbourne, biting the head off of a bat

01 = OA = Ophan Annie, sweeping-up

02 = OB = Obi-Wan Kenobi, switching on Light-sabre

03 = OC = Olivia Cooke, using ouija board (from movie)

04 = OD = Drug-user, shooting-up

05 = OE = Omar Epps, looking at X-rays (House & E.R.)

06 = OS = Omar Sharrif, playing Bridge

07 = James Bond (007), pointing pistol

08 = OH Oliver Hardy, spinning around with a plank of wood

09 = ON = Oliver North, raising right hand to take an oath

10 = Tony Blair, kissing a baby

11 = Ballerina, doing a pirouette

12 = AB = Alexander (Graham) Bell, answering telephone

13 = AC = Al Capone, hiding money in pockets

14 = AD = Arthur Daley, selling a second-hand car

15 = AE = Albert Einstein, pouring into a test tube

16 = AS = Alan Sugar, firing someone

17 = AG = Ariana Grande, singing into microphone

18 = AH = Adolph Hitler, doing goose-step march

19 = Paul Hardcastle, playing the song "19" on a turntable

20 = BO Derek, running out of the sea in a bikini

21 = BA = Mr. T, breaking a Snickers bar in half!

22 = BB = Boris Becker, playing Tennis

23 = BC = Jesus (Before Christ), hanging on a Cross

24 = BD = Bob Dylan, playing a tambourine against leg

25 = BE = Billy Elliot, doing the splits in mid-air

26 = BS = Bart Simpson, riding on skateboard

27 = BG = Bob Geldof, begging for money

28 = BH = Benny Hinn, pushing people on the forehead

29 = BN = Benjamin Netanyahu, lighting Menorah

30 = CO = Conan O'Brien, running fingers through hair

31 = CA = Charles Atlas, struggling under weight of a globe

32 = CB = Charlie Brown, missing ball and falling

33 = CC = Charlie Chaplin, twirling cane

34 = CD = Charles Dickens, asking for more (Oliver Twist)

35 = CE = Clint Eastwood, chewing a cigar

36 = CS = Claudia Sheiffer, on catwalk

37 = CG = Che Guevara, on motorbike

38 = CH = Charlton Heston, as Ben Hur on Chariot

39 = CN = Chuck Norris, karate-chopping wood in half

40 = DO = Dominic O'Brien, dealing pack of cards

41 = DA = David Attenborough, feeding chimpanzee

42 = DB = David Bowie, applying make-up

43 = DC = David Copperfield, pulling rabbit out of hat

44 = DD = Donald Duck, flying whilst pulling shorts up

45 = DE = Dame Edna, crossing legs

46 = DS = Delia Smith, flipping a pancake

47 = DG = David Gower, playing cricket

48 = DH = Damon Hill, driving

49 = DN = David Niven, folding a Paper Tiger

50 = EO = Eyore, sticking tail on (Donkey)

51 = EA = Edwin Armstrong, tuning a radio

52 = EB = Eric Bristow, throwing a dart

53 = EC = Eric Clapton, playing Electric Guitar

54 = ED = ED the horse, eating from trough

55 = EE = Eddie the Eagle Edwards, skiing (badly!)

56 = ES = Ebeneezer Scrooge, counting coins

57 = EG = Eddie Griffin, snorting crack cocaine

58 = EH = Ernest Hemmingway, fishing

59 = EN = Edward Norton, thumping chest like Hulk

60 = SO = Shaquiel O'Neil, dunking

61 = SA = Sally Army member, on trombone

62 = SB = Seve Ballisteros, playing golf

63 = SC = Seb Coe running Olympic race

64 = SD = Steve Davis, playing Snooker

65 = SE = Steve Erwin, feeding a crocodile

66 = Bobby Moore, lifting-up World Cup

67 = SG = Sally Gunnell, jumping hurdles

68 = SH = Sherlock Holmes, looking through microscope

69 = SN = Sam Neil, being eaten by dinosaur

70 = GO = George Orwell, writing

71 = GA = Gerry Adams, throwing a hand-grenade

72 = GB = George Bush, reading upside-down

73 = Bruce Lee, doing flying kick (died in 1973)

74 = GD = Gerard Depadeu, sword fighting

75 = GE = Gloria Estefan, dancing

76 = GS = Graeme Souness, kicking up soccer ball

77 = GG = Graham Greene, unwrapping Brighton Rock

78 = GH = Goldie Hawn, saluting (as Private Benjamin)

79 = GN = Gamal Nasser, building pyramid

80 = HO = Santa (Ho! Ho! Ho!), giving out presents

81 = HA = Clown (Ha! Ha!), juggling

82 = HB = Halle Berry, climbing wall, as Cat Woman

83 = HC = Henry Cooper, boxing

84 = HD = Humpty Dumpty, falling and cracking open

85 = HE = Harry Enfield, waving paper money

86 = HS = Homer Simpson, eating doughnuts

87 = HG = H.G. Wells, sitting in time-machine

88 = HH = Hulk Hogan, flexing muscles

89 = HN = Horatio Nelson, wearing eye patch / telescope

90 = NO = Nick Offerman, chopping wood with axe

91 = NA = Neil Armstrong, wearing space suit

92 = NB = Nora Batty, pulling up tights

93 = NC = Neville Chamberlain, giving Appeasement speech

94 = ND = Neil Diamond, playing the Piano

95 = NE = Noel Edmonds, being covered in gunk

96 = NS = Nigel Short, playing chess

97 = NG = Noel Gallagher, drinking a bottle of Beer

98 = NH = Nigel Havers, using stethoscope as doctor

99 = NN = Nannette Newman, washing-up

Believe me, I know that seems like a lot of work. It may seem like it is going to take a long time. Or it may even seem unachievable. I have experienced all of those thoughts and feelings and more beside. And I would humbly suggest that you are probably wrong.

The whole idea is to use associations that are quick and natural to you (and thus more likely to be remembered). For example, I do not really use Nick Offerman for the number 90 (the letters N and 0). I use someone I have known in my life who is very negative. I picture them pointing judgementally at someone and saying, "No!"

Also, I should say a word about the appropriateness of images here. And that word is – fugeddaboutit! For example, I have no reason to believe that Gerry Adams ever threw a Hand-grenade. However, as an English child my early life was spent hearing news reports about IRA bombings. And the news that I heard made almost zero distinction between Sein Fein and the IRA (at least, during the Troubles). So, although it may be neither Politically or historically correct to say that Gerry Adams threw hand-grenades (presumably for the IRA), it works as a memorable image for me.

As a further example, not being a fan, I have no idea if Neil Diamond even plays the Piano! Yet, I can see someone at a piano playing "Sweet Caroline," so that works for me.

It works to make your associations as unique and distinct as possible. Do not include too many e.g. Basketball players. I used to have a chess player and a memory competitor as characters of mine, but they both looked too alike in my very stereotypical memory images so I had to ditch one. That's another point to bear in mind – you want to exaggerate. (Have I not told you this a million times already?) Make that moustache extra bushy, amplify those biceps, shorten that skirt, increase that belly... the idea is to make something memorable as a reference you can easily and effortlessly bring to mind.

So, please, take my word for it and go and compile your list. Work with whatever association makes sense to your memory. Make them active, animated and unique.

Then come back here and we'll carry on.

How Do We Convert Numbers to Images?

You've done the hard work of compiling and memorising your 100 images. So, how do you use them? Well, let's recall our early 21-digit number to see just how simple this now becomes.

$$206631880710739731117$$

Using our list above, that would convert into the following 11 images:

Bo Derek, coming out of the Sea in a bikini

Bobby Charlton, lifting up the World Cup

A Fire-fighter, aiming his hose

Hulk Hogan, flexing his muscles

James Bond, spinning round and aiming a gun

Tony Blair, kissing a Baby

Bruce Lee, performing a flying kick

Noel Gallagher, drinking from a bottle

A Fire-fighter, aiming his hose

A Ballerina, performing a pirouette

7

(As you can see, we have a stray 7 at the end, but that is not a problem at all. The best option here is simply to convert it into one of the more static images from your number-rhyme or number-shape systems. The very fact it is not a person will alert you to the fact that it is a single digit and the end of the line.)

I'm sure you'll agree that those images are easier to remember than the 21-digit number. However, it may still seem a difficult task. This is where we return to the almighty method of Loci.

Think of an 11-stage journey. Any journey will do. I will think of a quick journey from my back garden to my front, without going upstairs:

1. Behind the back gate
2. In front of the gate, by the tree
3. On the Patio
4. Outside the double-doors
5. By the Television
6. On the Sofa
7. At the book-case

8. Sat at the Dining-room Table

9. In the kitchen : at the Sink

10. Bottom of the Stairs

11. Front Door

This list could have been much longer. There are numerous points I could have used. However, if you have read the chapter on Location, you know that already. The important thing is that this is the journey that will instantly and reliably occur to me as I run through the lower-floor of a house of mine.

And here is the practically effortless way that I use that journey – and my 100 people-with-actions – to recall a 21 digit number:

1. At my back gate: Bo Derek is running up to the gate in that famous yellow bikini of hers

2. Underneath the tree: Bobby Charlton lifts up the World Cup, as cheers go up from the birds in the branches

3. On the patio: A Fire-fighter is hosing down the patio

4. Looking through the double-doors: Hulk Hogan is flexing his muscles, desperately trying to impress

those inside

5. In front of the TV: Roger Moore as James Bond,
   spins round and aims a gun at those in the room

6. On the sofa: Tony Blair has the nerve to stand on
   my sofa, lifting up a baby to kiss like a scene from
   Lion King!

7. Book-case: Bruce Lee leaps through the air and
   kicks my book-case, knocking the books flying.
   Jerk!

8. Dining-room: Weirdly, Noel Gallagher is sat cross-
   legged on the table, drinking from a bottle. "Have
   you seen our kid?" he asks.

9. Kitchen sink: Rather than wait for the washing-up
   bowl to fill-up, a Fire-fighter aims water from his
   hose into the sink, sending water everywhere!

10. On the very last step of the stairs: A Ballerina
    performs a pirouette – and falls off the step.

11. Front Door: For some reason, I can not get out of
    the front door, because the door has been replaced
    by a great big scythe!

Now, running through that little movie in my mind, I
can confidently tell you that the 21 digit number that has
haunted us from the beginning of this book is: 20 66 31

88 07 10 73 97 31 11 7.

If you have done the work to devise your own 100-person-action list, even perhaps creating some journeys of your own, I am sure you will agree that memorising that 21-digit number – which may have seemed impossible before you began this book – was barely even a challenge.

It's actually really easy, right?

Can This Be Extended?

As it happens, it is possible to double the effectiveness of these 100 images. This is especially useful because it means we only need to come up with half as many locations for recall.

The way to increase your images is to use your person and actions as two separate associations. So, for example, at the moment 2193 might make us think of Mr. T. and also Neville Chamberlain (as two separate images, presumably requiring two separate locations). However, it is possible to create a complex image where the first two digits give us the person and the second two digits give us the action.

That would mean 2193 then converts into Mr. T. (the

person representing number 21) giving a speech (the action of number 93).

If the effectiveness of that extension does not appeal to you, then just ignore it. It is important not to feel overwhelmed by all you are learning, or your brain may just shut-down and reject even those parts that you already know are useful. However, if this make sense to you then you may already have realised that we could have pictured the above scene (which encodes a 21-digit number) in as little as 6 steps!

1. At my back gate: Bo Derek lifts up the World Cup
2. Under the tree: A Fire-fighter is flexing his muscles
3. On the patio: Roger Moore is lifting up a baby
4. In front of double-doors: Bruce Lee drinks a beer
5. In front of the TV: Fire-fighter does a pirouette
6. On the Sofa: A scythe cuts up numerous cushions

By now, you should be easily able to interpret that as: 2066 3188 0710 7397 3111 7

If all of that seems a step too far, then by all means move back a few stages. You do not need to extend your images in this way (known as a Person-Action list). Your basic 100-images will serve you just fine.

However, if this appeals to you, then can you imagine how effective it would be if you used a Person-Action-Person approach? You would then be recalling a 21 digit number as easily as this:

1. At my back gate: Bo Derk (Person 20) would be lifting (Action 66) a fire-fighter (Person 31).
2. Under the tree: Hulk Hogan (88) spins round (07) Tony Blair (10) !
3. On the patio: Bruce Lee (73) is drinking (97) a fire-fighter (31) - whatever that means in your imagination!
4. In front of double-doors: A Ballerina (11) interacts in some way with a Scythe! (7)

That's a 21 digit-number (206631 880710 739731 117) encoded easily in just 4 images. And it could have been 24 digits with hardly any extra effort!

I suspect that for most readers, this is far enough. We've geeked-out quite enough with numbers, for the time being. You may be convinced that they can be made memorable, but are happy working with just your 100 people for now, or at most a person-action list. Either way, you might enjoy reading the superfluous chapter coming up on memorising the first 100 digits of Pi.

However, before we indulge in that admittedly irrelevant exercise, let's apply this to memorising phone numbers.

How to Remember Phone Numbers

We can concentrate on mobile phone numbers here, as this is most likely what you will be dealing with. Either way, the process is the same.

So, let us imagine that we are tasked with remembering a fairly standard UK mobile phone number:

07205 956851

Obviously, the zero is unnecessary. So, this instantly becomes more manageable:

7205 9568 51

In practice, most mobile numbers in the UK start with 07. So, let's make this easier on ourselves and drop the 7 as well.[14] We are then left with:

---

14 Of course, as numbers increase, we will likely see more variety at the beginning of mobile phone numbers. It may therefore be useful to retain the 7, but move it to the end of the number (in this case, giving us 2059 5685

2059 5685 1

To remember this number, I would locate it in whichever place came to mind immediately. This might be where you first met the person the number belongs to, a location their name brings to mind, their work place, or even a location connected to where they live.

In this case, I will imagine that I met another parent at my child's birthday disco. So, I will place the action around the DJ's Sound Desk. To capture this number in that location, I would convert the numbers in the following way:

Person 20 + Action 59 + Person 56 + Action 85 + single digit 1.

The final digit is represented by a number taken from the Number Rhyme or Number Shape systems. The number 1 would give us either Bun (Number Rhyme) or Candle (Number Shape).

Thus, 2059-5685-1 becomes:

---

17). It may seem convoluted to reorganise numbers in this way, but it is to useful to avoid too much repetition. In short, numbers will be less memorable if they all start with the same limited series of digits.

- Robin Hood smashing
- Ebeneezer Scrooge waving a stash of paper money
- Bun / Candle

So, I picture this as:

Robin Hood picks up one of the speakers and smashes it onto the ground. On the other side of the DJ's deck, Ebeneezer Scrooge's is waving cash around. He looks round at the commotion, just as a pole (representing the number 1) from the DJ's sound system topples over and impales him (or his wad of cash, if you are less inclined to picture violent scenes).

The first PA and second PA are more memorable if linked in some way. However, simply placing them in the same, or adjacent, location – and ideally having them interact with that location in some way – effectively supports recall.

Alternatively, the first Person may be performing their Action on the second Person, as they carry out their action. That would give us:

Robin Hood picking up one of the speakers and smashing it onto Ebeneezer Scrooge's head as he waves his cash around. His head squishes like a large bun!

Perhaps we would benefit from a less violent example? I might have a client named Gordon, who immediately makes me think of Gordon Ramsey. He tells me that his mobile number is 07533 812515.

I shorten this to 5338 1251 5 and employ the following images:

- Eric Clapton whipping (as if on a chariot)
- Alexander Graham Bell tuning a radio
- Bee-hive / Sea-horse

This time, we will adapt the usual Person-Action approach to incorporate the final digit into the previous action. So, in effect, the final person will be performing their action with or upon the final digit. (In the previous example, that would have involved Ebeneezer Scrooge waving around a candle or bun, instead of wads of cash!)

We are then left with something like the following, taking place in a Restaurant Kitchen:

Eric Clapton whips Alexander Graham Bell, who is trying to tune a sea-horse.

I know, I promised something less violent this time around! So, we could adjust the action for 38 (riding a chariot), giving us:

Eric Clapton riding on the back of Alexander Graham Bell, who is bent over trying to tune-out the buzzing in a bee-hive!

As always, images are more memorable if you concoct them yourself. However, that may be stuck in my mind for quite some time!

Memorising Processes

Most of what follows in this book should by now be fairly obvious. However, I am including it to further demonstrate the effectiveness and applicability of memory tools. This applies, in particular, to the mesmerisingly powerful method of loci.

So, let us turn our attention now to how you might memorise specific therapeutic processes. We will start with one of the most popular inductions employed by hypnotists throughout the world. (An induction, for the non-hypnotic amongst my readers, is the process used to guide someone into an experience of hypnosis.) The following induction was developed and taught by Dave Elman and as such is usually referred to as the Elman Induction.

The Elman Induction

The steps of the Elman Induction are commonly taught

as:

- Pre-talk
- Eye-lock
- Deepener
- Fractionation
- Arm-drop
- Losing the Numbers

However, as argued by Larry Elman, son of the induction's inventor, this is an inaccurate and unhelpful way to frame things.[15] Larry Elman suggests that it is more useful to see the induction as following this order:

- Pre-talk
- Catalepsy of a group of small muscles (to bypass critical faculty)
- Deepening
- Fractionation
- Catalepsy of a group of large muscles
- Amnesia by suggestion

---

15 See Larry Elman, *Blueprint of the Dave Elman Induction*. This is further explored in my book, *The Elman Induction*.

We will remember these steps by taking a tour of a typical living-room. This room might include the following six features:

1. Arm-chair
2. Book-case
3. Television
4. Window
5. Picture
6. Stereo

As usual, using your own familiar locations is more effective, but this will serve us well for demonstration purposes.

If I was attempting to recall the steps of the Elman Induction, using this 6-stage 'journey,' I might do so as follows:

1. There is a PREacher standing on the arm-chair, giving a TALK about the dangers of hypnosis

2. Sitting on the top of my book-case is a well-known television CRITIC, stroking a kitten, surrounding by a group of similarly small CATs

3. A DEEP Sea Diver jumps into my TV and sinks inside

4. Matt Damon (playing his character from *Good Will Hunting*) is working out FRACTIONS in marker pen on the window pane

5. A muscular Tiger (or similar Large CAT) is attempting to knock my picture off the wall, leaving enormous scratches on the wall as he does so

6. Dominic O'Brien (who make me think of Memory, which reminds me to think of amnesia!) is ruining my record collection, by scratching LPs on the Record Player

Now, presuming you can recall my specific route around the room, I would be surprised if you could not immediately and effortlessly retrace my steps and locate each item from the induction in order. It could hardly be any easier, could it?

Fast Phobia Cure

Let's demonstrate this again, using a popular NLP technique, often referred to these days as the Fast Phobia Cure.[16] Here is how the steps of that technique might be executed:

1. Imagine you are sitting in a middle row of a Cinema.

In front of you is a screen which is far away from your position. In a moment, the movie of your experience is going to play on this screen, from before the fearful experience, right up until you were calm again.

2. Behind you is the Projection Booth, with all the controls.

Leave your body in the middle row and mentally float out of your seat and up into the projection booth. From the projection booth, you can watch yourself sitting in the middle row watching the screen.

---

16 It should not need stating - but I will do so any way – what follows is for the purposes of demonstrating a memory technique only. This is not offered as a means of learning the Fast Phobia Cure.

3. Run through the movie in fast forward, in black and white, freezing it when you reach the calm state at the end of the movie.

4. Now float out of the projector booth and enter your body sat in the middle row. Observe the calm at the end of the movie.

5. Float out of your body and go into the last scene which is still frozen in black and white.

6. Reverse the movie in colour from end to start, in just a matter of seconds.

7. Float back to your seat in the middle row.

8. Play the movie in fast forward again, in black and white, watching it from your seat. Freeze it when you reach the calm state at the end.

9. Float out of your body and go into the last scene which is still frozen in black and white.

10. Reverse the movie in colour from end to start, in

just a matter of seconds.

11. Repeat steps 8 to 11 another two or three times.

12. Break state and then test the response, by having them recall the scene that initially caused them distress.

To easily place these steps in a journey, as we did with the Elman induction, we will symbolise each step with a memorable image. For me, the following images spring to mind:

1. Cinema Seat
2. Movie Projector
3. Someone running in black and white
4. A ghost (i.e. a spirit possessing someone's body)
5. An ice sculpture (i.e. a black & white frozen statue)
6. A rainbow fading from the end to the beginning
7. Ghost relaxing in a cinema seat
8. Black & white runner
9. Ice sculpture
10. Rainbow fading
11. The Empire State Building breaking in two
12. Someone sitting an exam

Of course, you need to ensure that these images make you think of the relevant steps accurately and automatically. For me, #3 is Jesse Owens, the Olympic Runner, whom I have only seen in black and white. #4 is Linda Blair, from *The Exorcist* film. This is useful to distinguish it from the ghost in #7 (which is Casper, relaxing in a chair), where there is no element of entering another body.

To memorise these 12 steps, we can use a simple journey derived from the months of the year. You can, of course, use any 12-stage journey or palace. I am including this example to demonstrate how journeys can be found in all sorts of 'places.'

For me, the calendar provides the following 12-stages. It may be a stretch to call this a journey, as until you have rehearsed them a number of times they may not automatically follow in sequence. Perhaps think of them as peg locations?

January – I think of an extremely busy Department Store during the hideous January Sales. If that association does not work for you, you might think of someone you know called Jan, or Jane and picture their house or place of work.

February – The Eiffel Tower on Valentine's Day

March – A Bandstand (i.e. Marching band)

April – A joke shop (April Fools day)

May – Theresa May in the House of Commons (U.K.)

June – Sand dunes (or a scene from the movie *Dune*)

July – Julie's house (an old colleague of mine)

August – Augustus Gloop in a Chocolate river

September – The Twins Towers (9/11)

October – I imagine the Nursing Home where I used to visit my Octogenarian Grandmother

November – Fireworks display (Nov. 5th)

December – Christmas tree

Memorising the 12-steps of the Fast Phobia Cure we listed above should now cause you no difficulty at all. I would proceed in this manner:

1. I walk into a Department Store to see that all of the tills have been replaced by enormous comfy Cinema seats.

2. I am trying to propose to my partner at the top of the Eiffel Tower. However, onlookers are filming us on

large projectors and my fiance-to-be seems blinded by the light being shone in their eyes.

3. Jesse Owens is running round and round the bandstand in the town centre, perhaps clashing cymbals as he does so.

4. Linda Blair is in a joke shop trying on a clown's outfit, presumably having mistaken which horror movie franchise she represents!

5. Politicians in the House of Commons jeer as a frozen Theresa May fails to answer their questions.

6. On the set of the film, *Dune*, a large rainbow painted on the sand begins to fade/blow away from the end to the beginning.

7. Casper the friendly ghost is sat in a large chair on Julie's front porch, with a bag of popcorn.

8. Eric Liddell is being swept-along a chocolate river, weighed down by his gold medal.

9. At the foot of the Twins Towers, an enormous frozen Cross is melting, dripping onto the heads of those attempting to enter a building below.

10. Round the table at my late Grandmother's Nursing Home are a series of residents wearing jumpers in different colours of the rainbow. One by one, they fade away until only one elderly person in red is left!

11. At the usual site of my childhood school firework displays, someone has erected a statue of the Empire State Building, instead of a "guy."

12. In front of the enormous Rockefeller Center Christmas Tree, I picture a former client of mine who came to see me for exam nerves. Although their issue was resolved, for the purposes of being more memorable, I see them sat at a desk shaking in fear, sweating, scratching their head and looking round nervously, as shoppers rush passed them noisily destroying any hope they had of concentrating on their exam.

In all honesty, this may not be the best example to use, as it includes repetition and is often already situated in a specific location. However, it has been purposefully chosen to demonstrate the flexibility that can be employed to remember whatever information you need to retain.

It might seem more natural to use a journey around an actual cinema. I would caution against this, as it can lead to cross-contamination with the steps in the process you are aiming to memorise. There is no reason, however, that you could not use e.g. an open-air cinema, or even an old Blockbuster Video store, if you remember such things! That would give you a useful link with the cinema location frequently employed in the technique.

As we have seen a number of times now, flexibility and creativity are your friend. For example, if your journey involves two ghosts, serving different functions, you are not obliged to use the same character or image each time. You might even use the Priest from *The Exorcist*, or even Patrick Swayze (from *Ghost*), or [Spoiler alert!] Bruce Willis (from *Sixth Sense*).

If you do not know anyone called Julie, how about a "Jolly" friend, or someone whose birthday falls in July? You could even picture a gigantic Swimming Pool sized bowl of Jelly! August might inspire some kind or Roman landmark that Augustus Caesar makes you think of. October could involve a scene from the *Octopussy* film.

So, if my locations were memorable enough for you, or you used your own, how easily can you now recall the steps of the Fast Phobia Cure?

Memorising Scripts

We turn now to a part of the book that I have already been reliably informed will be welcome to many practitioners of hypnosis. Many hypnotherapists rely on scripts to remind them what suggestions they would like to pass on to their clients.

At the very least, they may use a script as a structure, or framework, from which to work. This latter approach seems preferable to me, though I recognise that we all have our own ways of working.

I am going to include an entire script here, taken from my book, *Use Hypnosis to Overcome Blushing*. This will take up a fair amount of space, but I felt that was useful to convey how effective this relatively simple technique can be.

***

Induction
So, you can begin by getting yourself

comfortable. And you can shift around to get even more comfortable any time you choose...

As we start, you can go ahead and take a nice deep breath... and then let it go. And again... and let it go.

And as you continue in that way, you can imagine breathing-in peace and comfort... and letting go of any stress and tension. Each breath in and out allowing you to drift more easily into that relaxation that you are beginning to enjoy.

I am sure you have had the experience of drifting into what hypnotists might call "trance." For many people, it may be sitting at the beach, watching the waves, as they come in and go out again... You can even get that experience, you know, just from watching fish in a tank, watching them silently swim by, this one, then that one.

Or perhaps you have sat in front of a log-fire, seeing the golden-orange flames flickering, as you listen to the crackling of the wood and feel more and more relaxed...

And sometimes, with experiences like that, you may lose all track of time... You might spend 10 minutes there, but it feels like an hour, or an hour and it feels just like 10 minutes.

Some people have a similar experience when they are driving. If they are driving a route they know well, you can have the unusual experience of reaching your destination and having no idea how you got there... It is as if your conscious mind takes a back seat, as your unconscious comes to the front.

And as we continue on, you may remember times in your life when you're lost in a daydream. At times, your conscious mind goes off and does its own thing, leaving you free to enjoy this experience. And someone could be calling your name, but you're just too far away to pay any attention. At other times, you have the same experience, but you could hear a pin drop. The important thing is not how you have that experience. The important thing is simply that you enjoy the dream.

And as you become aware of just how good it feels to close your eyes... and notice the tension leaving your body, just allowing that tension to flow away from you as every muscle relaxes... you can allow your mind to settle on a previous trance experience that you have had. It may be laying in a hammock, getting lost in a good book, fishing by a quiet river, meditating calmly, or a previous experience of hypnosis... Every fibre relaxing... As your mind relaxes too.

Just letting go and drifting off... deep into that comfortable heaviness of arms...of legs...of the whole body as you discovered just how easy... so pleasant... it can be to allow those feelings to continue... to deepen even more as you listen to the sound of my voice.

And as you recall that earlier experience... remembering that ability you have to let go completely and be totally unconcerned that there is no need at all for you to be concerned about how much effort it takes... to make an effort to try to hear or to understand everything that I say here or don't say there... so much easier to just let go and allow all of those things to occur in their own time and in their own way... and I know that you can cooperate with the whole process so well... that you can relax in that way... drifting down in that place inside... where all is still... quiet, peaceful... where there is only the sound of my voice and the wisdom that is your unconscious... as you become more... and more relaxed... nothing bothers you... nothing concerns you... as you continue to relax... to go deeper than before... each word that I say relaxing you... deeper... deeper... deeper.

As you continue now you can be aware too of the sound of my voice speaking to you here... as you relax so completely there... each word that I say a signal for you to relax... to let go... to drift even deeper now... You may or may not continue to be aware of the sounds that surround you... the sounds in the room... the ticking of the clock... all of those signs that remind you what a natural process this is... and how natural it is for you to return to that place.

And I wonder if you can allow that previous experience to continue here now... or to deepen even more as I continue to speak to you... my words drifting... as you drift too into comfortable relaxation of mind... relaxation of body... heaviness of arms... of legs... of no concern to you now... safe and secure... there for you when you need them... but for now they can rest... relax... relax in that comfortable place... deep inside... nothing bothers you or disturbs you as you continue now to use the power of your unconscious for your own good.

Staircase Deepener

As you sit there... comfortable and relaxed – you can imagine in front of you a staircase - a beautiful staircase with a polished, ornate banister running down alongside the staircase and a deep, rich carpet underneath your bare feet... As you look down the stairs you notice that there are ten steps leading gently down - ten steps... leading down, and down, and down.

These are the steps that will lead you deep into dream-time - deep into relaxation - and in a moment I'd like you to walk down those steps with me... and as we count them down you can notice that the deeper down you go, the more comfortable and the more relaxed you become.

At the bottom of the staircase, there is a large door – you may or may not notice what colour it is - with a door-knob for opening.

So when you are ready to walk down the stairs, gently place your hand on the banister... and begin to slowly descend the stairs as we count them off from 10 to 1.

[Say each number as they breathe out.]

10 – relaxed and comfortable

9 - deeper relaxed, deeper comfort

8 - more and more and more relaxed

7 - deeply relaxed, deeply comfortable

6 – nearly half way there

5 - more and more and more relaxed

4 - deeply relaxed, deeply comfortable

3 - more and more and more relaxed

2 - almost at the bottom now, just one more step to go, and...

1 - going deeper and deeper down into that relaxing experience, to that deeper, healthier level of mind.

And as you reach the bottom step, you can allow the ordinary cares and worries of the everyday world to stay back there... as you drift deeper and deeper into that relaxation.

As you are standing at the bottom of the steps... comfortable, relaxed and at peace with the world... you can see that large door in front of you. The door is closed, but there's a large door knob easily within reach. And you really want to go through the door and see what is there on the other side, for you somehow know that a wonderful place is there waiting for you.

So move now toward the door. Twist the door knob. Push it open. Push the door open... The door creaks gently open, and you push it even further open and walk through.

Now close the door behind you and turn and find yourself in a very special place. This is *your* special place... a place of peace and calm, safety and serenity.

Special Place

Take some time to acquaint yourself with your surroundings... Take in the peace, the calm and serenity... Breathe it in. Enjoy it.

You might notice any sights or sounds that you did not expect to encounter, perhaps the sound of birds singing, or children laughing, or colours which seem particularly prominent... Simply allow yourself to see what you see, hear what you hear and feel whatever you feel.

After a while, I would like you to notice anywhere that you can go to sit down, or lay down and relax... This might be a park bench, a towel on the sand, or just sitting against a tree, under the shade of its branches.

Now, go ahead and sit down or lay down and relax.

Confidence Anchor

Noticing now that the deeper you go, the better you feel and the better you feel the deeper you will go with every breath that you take, every noise that you hear and every word that I say... as you now allow your mind to wander free as you continue to go deeper down into the world of your dreams and the world of your imagination... I want you to imagine and remember a time in your life when you felt confident. And see a movie of that scenario where you are confident. Notice how you stand, how you carry yourself. Perhaps you can tell that you are feeling confident just by watching. And we can feel confident for any number of reasons... It can be because we know what we're doing, or we feel good about ourselves, or we just feel comfortable and competent in the setting we are in. Whatever the reason, notice what the confident you looks like... And I'd like you to imagine a golden almost aura surrounding that you, a confident glow.

And when you can see that, go and step into that confident you... Feel what it feels like to be so confident. Wear that aura and feel that confidence flowing around you. Be filled from head to toe with that confidence... And when you can feel that confidence filling you now, you can go ahead and push together the tip of your forefinger of the right hand together with the tip of your thumb and this will make your ring of confidence. And when that confidence reaches its peak, you can let it go.

Now, perhaps you can recall another time when you felt confident. And see yourself there, all full of confidence, surrounded again by that aura. Notice what you look like when you are confident, and how you sound. And go ahead and step into that confident you and wear that aura as you are filled with confidence from head to toe. Get a good feel for what it feels like to be so full of confidence... And when you can feel that here and now, go ahead and make that ring of confidence again, almost as if you are locking-in that confidence as a resource for whenever you need it. And when that confidence reaches its peak, you can let it go.

Now, for a third time, recall another occasion when you felt confident. And see yourself there, full of confidence, surrounded by that aura. Notice what you look like when you are confident, and how you sound... Go ahead and step into that confident you and wear that aura as you are filled with confidence from head to toe. Get a good feel for what it feels like to be so full of confidence... And when you can feel that here and now, go ahead and make that ring of confidence, locking-in that confidence for whenever you need it. And when that confidence reaches its peak, you can let it go.

You can know now that whenever you need to call upon these feelings in your every day life, whenever you are facing the kind of situations that might have previously caused you to blush, then now as an automatic reflex action all you need do is push together the tip of your forefinger of the right hand together with the tip of your thumb and instantly this will make your ring of confidence, bringing all those confident feelings back to you as you are surrounded by that aura and filled with that confidence... And your subconscious can remind you as an automatic reflex action to make this ring of confidence with your finger and thumb as and when you need it in your everyday life.

In fact, you can go ahead and picture a scene in the future that may have caused you to blush in the past. And the second – the very second – you feel anything like those old feelings, you can squeeze that finger and thumb together, be filled with confidence and feel that confidence flowing around you... Notice how different you are, how more engaged and relaxed you are, when you allow yourself to be this confident you.

That's right.

Autogenic Training

And as you allow your attention to move to your right hand now, you can say in your head, "My hands are warm and heavy... my hands are warm and heavy..." And use your imagination as you do so, to experience what you are describing. "My hands are warm and heavy..." feeling them getting warmer, heavier. "My hands are warm and heavy..."

And as you concentrate on those sensations, I wonder if you bring to mind resting in front of a log-fire, warming up your hands... And as you focus on that experience, you will notice that you really can feel your hands getting warmer... And as your hands get warmer, you drift further into that restful relaxation, and as you drift further into that rest, your hands continue to warm up. Perhaps you rub your hands together, really feeling that warmth, before you place them in front of the fire again... And as those hands get warmer, it is almost as if they give off a red glow, a fiery red pulsating glow of warmth.

The thing that is particularly interesting is that just as you can warm-up your hands, you can cool them down. I wonder if you are able to recall playing in snow as a child. Perhaps you are making a snowman, or you're having a snowball fight. And if you are anything like me, you may have stayed out in the snow way past the point when you were too cold to be there. Maybe your gloves are too thin, or perhaps you've taken them off to get a better grip on the snow, but you can feel the freezing temperatures against your skin… And as you recall that sensation now, you may also be able to imagine two buckets full of ice. And you can dive your hands into those buckets, feeling that sudden and definite change in temperature, as your hands get colder now. And as they get really cold, and you can feel that, it may almost seem as if they turn a pale blue.

And then you can take them out, dry them with a towel and return to the warmth of your special place.

Not being self-conscious

I can remember an event that brings me great amusement now, but it may have troubled me in the past. I was walking home from the gym one day, when a toddler was walking past with his mum. And he saw me and pointed and smiled. I smiled back, because who can resist the smile of a toddler? And then he surprised me by saying, "big fat man!" I laughed and went on my way.

Now, some time ago, a statement like that may have bothered me. If I was feeling self-conscious or fragile, it might have got to me. However, the toddler did not see the whole picture… The toddler did not know, for example, that I was coming back from the gym, feeling full of the endorphins that a good work-out gives you. He also did not know that I had lost 4 stone in the previous year and was feeling great about how my weight was going down… And he did not know that I had a child the same age at home and I knew that they often said things that just popped into their head, with no malice or evil intent whatsoever.

The fact is, I *was* overweight. And that toddler had presumably heard someone who looked like me being called a "big fat man." So, he saw me and recalled that previous experience. But I was not the slightest bit bothered by what he had to say… I felt good about myself, felt positive about my weight that happened to be going down and either way I was a grown man who wasn't inclined to get upset by something a toddler said!

People do not always see the whole picture.

There's a story from *The Seven Habits of Highly Effective People* by Steven Covey. He speaks of being on a subway train in New York one Sunday morning.

People were sitting quietly – some reading newspapers, some lost in thought, some resting with their eyes closed. It was a calm, peaceful scene... Then suddenly, a man and his children entered the subway car. The children were so loud and rambunctious that instantly the whole climate changed.

The man sat down next to Covey and closed his eyes, apparently oblivious to the situation. The children were yelling back and forth, throwing things, even grabbing people's papers. It was very disturbing. And yet, the man sitting next to Covey did nothing.

It was difficult not to feel irritated. People couldn't believe that he could be so insensitive as to let his children run wild like that and do nothing about it, taking no responsibility at all. It was easy to see that everyone else on the subway felt as irritated as Covey. So finally, he turned to him and said, "Sir, your children are really disturbing a lot of people. I wonder if you couldn't control them a little more?"

The man looked-up, as if he was becoming aware of the situation for the first time. And he said softly, "Oh, you're right. I guess I should do something about it... We just came from the hospital where their mother died about an hour ago. I don't know what to think, and I guess they don't know how to handle it either."

When you know the full picture about yourself - how strong you have been to face and overcome this issue that was a problem for so many years – it is easier to be unaffected by the things that other people say, do or think... And, of course, there is always the saying that we would be less affected by what other people think of us if we realised how rarely they do.

We are all just busy getting on with our lives, doing the best we can.

Picture scene where warm changed to cold

And I wonder if you can picture another scene that would have previously caused you to blush. And see what happens the minute you feel any warmth in those cheeks. You can simply say in your head, "My hands are warm and heavy." And allow that warmth to flow down to your hands. And as that warmth leaves your face, it can leave behind a nice pale blue fresh chill in its place.

Picture scene without being self-conscious

And in those situations where you used to blush, either the one you've just thought of, or another, you can pay attention to the person talking to you, without wondering or worrying what they are thinking about you. You are confident and secure in yourself.

And you can watch the person who is talking to you and it might amuse you to think that they themselves could even be worrying what you are thinking about them. We just can't tell.

And as you are watching them, listening, engaging with the conversation, you can be one of those rare people who gives someone else the gift of 100% attention... And you can feel good about that.

Re-writing History

All of these things that you have now learnt and this entire journey you have been on means that you can go back into your past, to every time when you used to blush and re-write it... You can fill each scene with self-confidence, knowing that you only need to press your finger and thumb together to be surrounded and filled with confidence... Maybe moving onto the next scene, you are not overly self-conscious, as you focus instead on the person in front of you. On to another scene, when you feel physical warmth in your cheeks, you send it down to your hands and your cheeks become cool.

And you can allow your subconscious mind to move through your personal history – able to do so much more quickly than your conscious mind – re-writing your story... You are no longer a blusher. You are someone who used to blush.

And if, in the future, you ever do find your cheeks going slightly red, you can find that amusing as it reminds you of that old issue that you've overcome... Now, you simply experience that occasional tinge that all people do from time to time. Blushing is no longer a problem for you. It no longer defines who you are.

Re-emergence

And now, just as quickly as your conscious mind and subconscious can agree to work together to implement all of the changes that you have experienced here today, you can slowly, in your own time, open your eyes feeling revitalised and refreshed.

***

Substituting the Script

You may be well ahead of me here, but the first step is to select the major points, key ideas and any shifts, movements, or turning-points in the script. We will then convert them into memorable images. I will demonstrate this at length, so apologies to those of you who can already see what this would look like!

As you look back over our script, you may well select different points to me. For example, you may only need to keep the word "Staircase" to remind you of the whole section under the heading Staircase Deepener. Others, like I have below, might want to remind themselves to count each number as their client exhales. Similarly, you might want to include more or less detail than I have from the Confidence Anchor section.

You will note that I keep the headings in as specific points to recall. Personally, I find this helpful to give me an idea for where I am in the flow of the script.[17] Additionally, if there are certain phrases that I want to use and repeat verbatim, I make a point of highlighting them and making a specific image for them.

In reality, if I was memorising this script, I would work to cut it down to 26 stages. Over the years, I have devised numerous 26-stage journeys to choose from and I am just stubborn these days – and perhaps a little superstitious! – about squeezing anything and everything into them. As it is, to demonstrate how you may want to proceed, I have selected 42 key-points from the script. See if you would have chosen the same parts to highlight.

1. INDUCTION
2. breathing-in peace
3. the experience of drifting into what hypnotists might call "trance" : beach, fish, log-fire

---

17 You may choose to differentiate a heading in some way, e.g. enlarge it, display it on a billboard, etc. However, I keep it as a normal image, but ensure that nothing else is taking place.

4. lose all track of time, driving

5. daydream

6. The important thing is simply that you enjoy the dream.

7. become aware of just how good it feels to close your eyes...

8. notice the tension leaving your body

9. allow your mind to settle on a previous trance experience that you have had... As your mind relaxes too.

10. Just letting go and drifting off... allow those feelings to continue...

11. STAIRCASE DEEPENER

12. At the bottom of the staircase, there is a large door – you may or may not notice what colour it is - with a door-knob for opening.

13. So when you are ready to walk down the stairs, gently place your hand on the banister... and begin to slowly descend the stairs as we count them off from 10 to 1.

14. [Say each number as they breathe out.]

15. SPECIAL PLACE

16. Take some time to acquaint yourself with your surroundings...

17. You might notice any sights or sounds that you did not expect to encounter

18. Now, go ahead and sit down or lay down and relax.

19. CONFIDENCE ANCHOR

20. imagine a golden almost aura surrounding that you

21. step into that confident you... Be filled from head to toe with that confidence...

22. make your ring of confidence... x3

23. picture a scene in the future that may have caused you to blush in the past.

24. AUTOGENIC TRAINING

25. "My hands are warm and heavy..."

26. resting in front of a log-fire, warming up your hands...

27. recall playing in snow as a child

28. return to the warmth of your special place

29. NOT BEING SELF-CONSCIOUS

30. "Big fat man!"

31. *The Seven Habits of Highly Effective People*. being on a subway train. The children were so loud and rambunctious. their mother died.

32. know the full picture about yourself - how strong you have been – it is easier to be unaffected by the things that other people say, do or think...

33. PICTURE SCENE WHERE WARM CHANGED TO

COLD

34. And allow that warmth to flow down to your hands. And as that warmth leaves your face, it can leave behind a nice pale blue fresh chill in its place.

35. PICTURE SCENE WITHOUT BEING SELF-CONSCIOUS

36. pay attention to the person talking to you, without wondering or worrying what they are thinking about you. You are confident and secure in yourself.

37. it might amuse you to think that they themselves could even be worrying what you are thinking about them.

38. RE-WRITING HISTORY

39. fill each scene with self-confidence

40. On to another scene, when you feel physical warmth in your cheeks, you send it down to your hands and your cheeks become cool.

41. You are someone who used to blush.

42. RE-EMERGENCE

If you feel that you would have chosen more or fewer key-points to select, that is of course your choice. In reality, I suspect that if you simply chose to substitute the headings with memorable images, combined with reading through the script a number of times, you would remember most (if not all) of the script fairly effortlessly. For those of you choosing to do that, there are conveniently 10 headings, which would no doubt be a simple task for you to memorise by this point.[18]

Nevertheless, I will endeavour to capture the preceding 42 points using a journey from an early house of mine to my first place of full-time employment. The journey is relatively straightforward:

1. Bedroom
2. Top of Stairs
3. Attic
4. 2nd Bedroom
5. Bathroom
6. Bottom of Stairs
7. Living Room
8. Kitchen
9. Dining Room
10. Bushes outside house
11. Trees at end of Bowmer Street

---

18 I should perhaps clarify that the goal is not to repeat the script verbatim. That is rarely a good idea and clients can often tell when you are doing so. The point is to capture the main points, gist and flow, using the script like a framework, with pointers to key ideas.

12. Bowmer Street sign

13. Wilmorton Off-Licence

14. Bus Stop (Inside the bus)

15. School House

16. Bargain Bikes

17. Bus Shelter (Left)

18. Hand Car wash (Left)

19. Pub toilets (on Right)

20. Business Park's massive three trees (Right)

21. Car Park Barrier (Right)

22. Top of bridge (middle of road)

23. Mamma Mia's Takeaway

24. Arches between shops

25. Adult Bookshop (Left)

26. Royal Mail Sorting Centre

27. Newspaper seller (by monument)

28. Train Station drop-off point

29. Taxi ranks

30. Station ticket office (inside on left)

31. Massage Parlour

32. Pool Hall

33. Brunswick Inn mini car park

34. Underpass

35. Steps alongside River

36. River Bridge (half way across)

37. Benches

38. Old Silk Mill

39. Outside Wesley Owen

40. Cathedral

41. Cathedral Cafe and Bookshop

42. The Standing Order Pub

Obviously, that route will not mean much to you, unless you happen to know the City of Derby in the UK. However, as I describe the following scenes, imagine them as effectively as you can – remembering the principles of SMASHIN' SCOPE – and I think you will be surprised how much of the script you can later recall.

1. Bedroom

Induction

I picture a baby being induced right in the middle of my bed. It's loud. It's graphic. It's making a mess of the bedding that I just changed this morning!

2. Top of Stairs

breathing in peace

I see a stereotypical hippie from the 60's laying across the top of the stairs. In fact, I cannot get passed him, because he's sprawled out, inhaling deeply from a bong. There is a large Peace symbol on his t-shirt. There is a strong smell of, well, incense.

3. Attic

the experience of drifting into what hypnotists might call "trance" : beach, fish, log-fire

The entrance to the attic is in the ceiling between the two bedrooms. As I poke my head through the hatch to the attic, I see an old room-mate of mine who used to listen to Trance music. He's dancing in an ecstatic manner to the cacophony he calls music. I step-up into the attic and am surprised to see that the whole right-hand side of it has been covered in sand, with large fish jumping out of the water beyond that. On the far side of this make-shift beach, people warm themselves by a fire. It crackles, spits and sputters. Someone is cooking one of the fish which presumably leapt a little too high!

4. 2nd Bedroom

lose all track of time, driving

All of the furniture has been removed from the 2nd bedroom to make room for an unusually large Scalextric track. Flavor Flav (from the group *Public Enemy*) is sitting on one of the cars, with his iconic clock hanging from his neck, the hands going in all kinds of directions. He flies off the track, as he approaches the corner too quickly.

5. Bathroom

daydream

Lying in the bath is a younger version of myself, dressed in my school uniform. I look adorable! I am wide-awake, but staring dreamily out of the window – as I was prone to do – twiddling the hair behind my ear.

6. Bottom of Stairs

The important thing is simply that you enjoy the

dream.

At the foot of the stairs, lies an exaggerated version of a friend's pet dog. It wags its tail as it dreams, periodically letting out what sounds like a contented sigh between its snoring.

7. Living Room

become aware of just how good it feels to close your eyes...

As I enter the living-room, the room appears to go dark and then light. It does that again and then again. I realise that my eyes are closing and opening, as I am feeling extremely tired. I sit on the sofa and allow my eyes to close. And it feels GOOD!

8. Kitchen

notice the tension leaving your body

I am annoyingly awakened by a loud booming voice coming from the kitchen. I open the door to see a Sgt.

Major yelling, "At-tention!" He turns and leaves the room when he sees me. I feel a tangible sense of relief as he disappears.

9. Dining Room

allow your mind to settle on a previous trance experience that you have had... As your mind relaxes too.

As I enter the dining-room, I see my old room-mate yet again. However, there are numerous iterations of him, each from different stages in my life when I have known him. I focus in on one version of him, from a few years ago, walk over and begin to dance with him.

10. Bushes outside house

Just letting go and drifting off... allow those feelings to continue...

I step out-side the front door, where I see Queen Elsa (from *Frozen*) standing next to a row of large bushes. Mysteriously, the bushes begin to float-up into the air. I try hard to hold on to the largest and heaviest of them, but – predictably enough – Elsa encourages me to "let it go!" I do so and as it continues to join the other bushes, I once again feel the relief I had felt in the kitchen.

11. Trees at end of Bowmer Street

Staircase Deepener

When I get to the end of my road, I see the border of trees to the left. Bizarrely, I see my old neighbours stood on the top of one of the trees, about to step onto an escalator that appears to take them down from the trees and into the ground.

12. Bowmer Street sign

At the bottom of the staircase, there is a large door – you may or may not notice what colour it is - with a door-knob for opening.

Next to the street sign, there is an enormous red door with a large brass door knob. It occupies the entire space previously taken by the house there. (I do not worry about remembering the staircase in this image, or the next, as I know we are in the Staircase Deepener section of the script due to the downward escalator.)

13. Wilmorton Off-Licence

So when you are ready to walk down the stairs, gently place your hand on the banister... and begin to slowly descend the stairs as we count them off from 10 to 1.

As I enter the Off-Licence on the corner of the street, holding on to the railing, I am greeted by the shocking sight of a large crowd of people counting, enthusiastically, "10! 9! 8! 7!" The scene is reminiscent of the fireworks along London's River Thames on New Year's Eve and I decide to exit the shop rather than find out what happens when they get down to number 1!

14. Bus Stop (Inside the bus)

[Say each number as they breathe out.]

I jump on the bus and when I take my seat, I look up to see my old Maths teacher leading all of the passengers in a series of breathing exercises.

15. School House

Special Place

As I pass the old School House, I see angels out-front, playing harps in a stereotypically heavenly scene. Only the occasional one is in the relevant school uniform – complete with cap – so it's not as weird as it could be!

16. Bargain Bikes

Take some time to acquaint yourself with your surroundings...

The bikes that are usually out the front of Bargain Bikes have been replaced by grandfather clocks. Inside the store, the other bikes have all been cleared to make room for someone who is unfolding an enormous map and checking a compass.

17. Bus Shelter (Left)

You might notice any sights or sounds that you did not

expect to encounter

At the Bus shelter, I am somewhat taken aback to see Roald Dahl[19] winding round a jack-in-the-box, which pops up to reveal Pavarotti. I certainly did not expect that!

18. Car wash (Left)

Now, go ahead and sit down or lay down and relax.

The Car wash is in full flow. However, for some reason there is not a car between the brushes, but someone laying on a massage table!

19. Pub toilets (on Right)

Confidence Anchor

I am about to enter one of the toilet cubicles, but discover that I cannot go inside because Ron Burgundy (a confident Anchorman) is sat on the toilet reading the headlines. Pull your trousers up, Ron!

------

19 Roald Dahl used to present the TV show, *Tales of the Unexpected.*

20. Business Park's massive three trees (Right)

imagine a golden almost aura surrounding that you

I see myself standing in front of the 3 trees outside the Business Park. An enormous pulsating gold ring encircles me and all three trees.

21. Car Park Barrier (Right)

step into that confident you... Be filled from head to toe with that confidence...

The Car Park barrier comes up to reveal someone gradually turning to gold (a la King Midas) from the top to the bottom.

22. Top of bridge (middle of road)

make your ring of confidence... x3

In the middle of the road, blocking all of the traffic at the top of the bridge, are 3 con-men (from the TV series, *The Hustle*) dancing in a circle and singing "Ring a ring of roses."

23. Mamma Mia's Takeaway

picture a scene in the future that may have caused you to blush in the past.

The entire front window of the takeaway has been replaced by a large portrait of the robot "Bender" (from *Futurama*) with a bright red face.

24. Arches between shops

Autogenic Training

Jennifer Anniston is dressed-up like she works in an Auto-repair shop. She is lifting a heavy barbell, apparently in training.

25. Adult Bookshop (Left)

"My hands are warm and heavy..."

Outside the adult bookshop is a large concrete

monument of a pair of gloves. Heat radiates off it and steam is rising into the air.

26. Royal Mail Sorting Office

resting in front of a log-fire, warming up your hands...

On the steps to the Sorting Office, I see a circle of Cub Scouts sat round a fire. They are singing camp-fire songs, whilst some heat marshmallows and others warm their hands.

27. Newspaper seller (by monument)

recall playing in snow as a child

Next to the monument is a Newspaper seller in his kiosk. He is normally calling to passer-bys. However, today, he is ducking down, dodging the snowballs that are repeatedly being thrown in his direction.

28. Train Station drop-off point

return to the warmth of your special place

We are back with the angels again. Only this time, they are dressed as if they are off on their Summer Holidays! Michael is wearing Bermuda Shorts, sunglasses and flip-flops. And you do not want to know what Gabriel is wearing!

29. Taxi ranks

Not being self-conscious

At the taxi rank, outside Derby Train Station, someone (possibly Robert De Niro from *Taxi Driver*?) is hiding their face behind a taxi wing mirror. Then they jump-up and confidently yell, "peekaboo!" without a care in the world.

30. Station ticket office (inside on left)

"Big fat man!"

Inside the Train Station, in front of the ticket office to the left, Mike Myer's character, "Fat Bastard" (from *Austin Powers in Goldmember*) is dancing as he chases a customer singing, "I want my baby back baby back baby back baby back baby back ribs. I want my baby back baby back baby back baby back baby back ribs."

31. Massage Parlour

The Seven Habits of Highly Effective People. being on a subway train. The children were so loud and rambunctious. their mother died

For some reason, I picture the Massage Parlour from the film, *40-Year Old Virgin*. Instead of 7 children, I picture the 7 Dwarves as characterised in the Disney Snow White film. I give them bad habits (mostly involving picking of some kind!) and they are each eating a subway sandwich. They are dressed in funeral clothes.

32. Pool Hall

know the full picture about yourself - how strong you have been – it is easier to be unaffected by the things that other people say, do or think...

Whilst people are trying to play a game of Pool, they have to contend with a Circus "Strong Man" who is paying careful attention to himself in a full-length mirror. He is oblivious to the players shouting at him to get out of the way.

33. Brunswick Inn mini car park

Picture scene where warm changed to cold

The tiny car park next to the Brunswick Inn pub is completely taken-over by a portable heater the size of a large tank! However, as it blows air out at the passing cars, it is clear that it is cold air, with a number of them turning to ice as a result!

34. Underpass

And allow that warmth to flow down to your hands. And as that warmth leaves your face, it can leave behind a nice pale blue fresh chill in its place

The Human Torch from the *Fantastic 4* is hovering in the Underpass. His head is on fire, but the flames gradually move down his arms until it is just his hands on fire. I look up and am surprised to see that his face is now blue.

35. Steps alongside River

Picture scene without being self-conscious

A group of people wearing Theatrical masks stand in front of portraits of themselves (as if they are mirrors). Is this some kind of "Flash mob"? I can't abide flash mobs! One by one, they remove their masks. I decide to be on my way before anything else happens.

36. River Bridge (half way across)

pay attention to the person talking to you, without wondering or worrying what they are thinking about you. You are confident and secure in yourself.

At the half-way point across the bridge, two people are blocking the walk-way, sat opposite each other in office chairs. One is deep in conversation and the other is listening intently. The person listening is wearing a Security jacket.

37. Benches

it might amuse you to think that they themselves could even be worrying what you are thinking about them.

At the next scene, another Security guard (for some reason, I see Bruce Willis from the film *Unbreakable*!) is rolled-up in a ball on the floor, laughing. People sat on the bench are looking around at each other anxiously, not sure which one of them Bruce is laughing at.

38. Old Silk Mill

Re-writing History

The *Old Silk Mill* pub used to have some wonderfully comfortable Sofas inside. However, one of the sofas has been replaced by an old school desk (the kind with the built-in ink wells). Sat at the desk is the historian Howard Zinn, striking-out and re-writing someone else's account of the history of the USA.

39. Outside Wesley Owen

fill each scene with self-confidence

Outside the Wesley Own book shop, Phil Mitchell is smugly filling boxes with pictures of himself!

40. Cathedral

On to another scene, when you feel physical warmth in your cheeks, you send it down to your hands and your cheeks become cool.

At the front of the Cathedral I am somewhat alarmed to see an effigy of myself on fire! The flames start at my head, but gradually move down my arms until it is just my hands on fire and my face is now ice-blue.

41. Cathedral Cafe and Bookshop

You are someone who used to blush.

In the Cathedral Cafe, I see a younger version of myself, complete with bright red cheeks. As I make eye-contact with myself, a smile spreads across my young face and my cheeks then return to their usual adorable pale pink.

42. The Standing Order Pub

Re-emergence

Tired from such an eventful journey, I enter The Standing Order for some liquid refreshment. As I approach the bar to order, I am taken aback to see Sleeping Beauty, in a glass casket, on the bar. As I approach to take a closer look, I see that she is waking-up and she does so with a stretch and a loud yawn.

And that's our journey complete!

That was not the only way we could have done that. You will see that I often created active scenes, more than merely static images. Some people might prefer to take their memorable phrase or idea and shorten it into just one or two cue-words. That word can then be pictured by a simpler image than many of the ones I used.

Hopefully you noticed the use of SMASHIN' SCOPE in coming up with many of the scenes I used. You may also have seen how I did not simply place each image or scene at the required location. The really memorable images will be those where the character or image interacted in some way with the location.

So, here is where the rubber hits the road. I do not necessarily expect you to remember the part of the script being referred to, but would it not be interesting to go back through the journey and see how many of those 42 images you can now recall?

Well, here's your chance!

1. Bedroom
2. Top of Stairs
3. Attic
4. 2nd Bedroom
5. Bathroom
6. Bottom of Stairs
7. Living Room
8. Kitchen
9. Dining Room
10. Bushes outside house
11. Trees at end of Bowmer Street
12. Bowmer Street sign
13. Wilmorton Off-Licence

14. Bus Stop (Inside the bus)
15. School House
16. Bargain Bikes
17. Bus Shelter (Left)
18. Hand Car wash (Left)
19. Pub toilets (on Right)
20. Business Park Three Trees (Right)
21. Car Park Barrier (Right)
22. Top of bridge (middle of road)
23. Mamma Mia's Takeaway
24. Arches between shops
25. Adult Bookshop (Left)
26. Royal Mail Sorting Centre
27. Newspaper seller (by monument)
28. Train Station drop-off point
29. Taxi ranks
30. Station ticket office (inside on left)
31. Massage Parlour
32. Pool Hall
33. Brunswick Inn mini car park
34. Underpass
35. Steps alongside River
36. River Bridge (half way across)
37. Benches
38. Old Silk Mill

39. Outside Wesley Owen

40. Cathedral

41. Cathedral Cafe and Bookshop

42. The Standing Order Pub

How did you get on? My guess is that you did better than you expected? I would also presume that those scenes that stuck the most firmly in your mind did so for one or more of the following reasons: i) the location was clear and distinct in the beginning, ii) you employed SMASHIN' SCOPE principles, iii) your image interacted with the location in some way.

I would like to make one more guess. My guess would be that if you read back through the journey we created, you would get 42 out of 42 next time. And if you re-read the script before doing that, you might really impress yourself with how much you can recall – and just how easy you find it!

Memorising Historic Dates

You will no doubt recall that when we first looked at the method of Loci, we used it to memorise the following list:

- Mesmerism

- Psychoanalysis

- Alfred Adler's Individual Psychology

- Carl Jung Analytical Psychology

- Rogers Client-Centred Therapy

- Gestalt Therapy

- Behavioural therapy (B. F. Skinner)

- Humanistic psychology (E.g. Maslow)

- Rational Emotive Behaviour Therapy

- Logotherapy

- Reality Therapy

- CBT

- Primal therapy

- SFBT

- ACT

- Narrative Therapy

Now, let's take this one step further and add some dates to these therapeutic breakthroughs.

1774 – Franz Anton Mesmer described the therapeutic properties of "animal magnetism" (hypnosis), and began his clinical practice.

1886 – Sigmund Freud begins offering therapy to patients in Vienna, Austria.

1911 – Alfred Adler left Freud's Psychoanalytic Group to form his own school of thought, *Individual Psychology*, accusing Freud of overemphasising sexuality and basing theories on his own childhood.

1913 – Carl Jung departed from Freud and developed

his own theories. His new school of thought became known as *Analytical Psychology*.

1951 – Carl Rogers published his major work, *Client-Centered Therapy*.

1951 – The seminal work of *Gestalt Therapy* is published, co-authored by Fritz Perls.

1953 – B.F. Skinner outlined behavioural therapy, lending support for behavioural psychology in *Science and Human Behaviour*.

1954 – Abraham Maslow helped to found *Humanistic Psychology* and later developed his famous Hierarchy of Needs.

1955 – Albert Ellis began teaching the methods of *Rational Emotive Behaviour Therapy,* arguably the first form of Cognitive Therapy.

1959 – Viktor Frankl published the first English edition of *Man's Search for Meaning*, which provided an existential account of his Holocaust experience and an overview of his system called *Logotherapy*.

1965 – William Glasser published *Reality Therapy*, describing his psychotherapeutic model and introducing his concept of Control Theory [later renamed to Choice Theory].

1967 – Aaron Beck published a psychological model of depression, suggesting that thoughts play a significant role in the development and maintenance of depression. Becks model came to be known as *Cognitive Behavioural Therapy*, or CBT.

1970 Arthur Janov published his book, *The Primal Scream*, which outlined his theory of trauma-based *Primal Therapy*.

1978 – Berg and de Shazer co-founded the Brief Family Therapy Center (BFTC) in Milwaukee, out of which *Solution-Focused Brief Therapy* was born.

1982 – Steve Hayes and colleagues develop *Acceptance and Commitment Therapy*.

1990 – Michael White and David Epston publish *Narrative Means to Therapeutic Ends*, the first major text in what later comes to be known as *Narrative Therapy*.

If you have read the chapter on memorising numbers, you will know what is coming next. To remember these dates we will convert the 4-digit date into a Person + Action and then associate that with the event to be recalled. Of course, one of the most effective means of associating the date and the event is through utilising locations.

The benefit of using locations is that we effectively have two ways in to our memorable image. We can recall the date and that will make us think of someone doing something somewhere – giving us the location and thus the event. Or, we can start with the event, which will give us a location where we will see someone doing something - providing us with the date.

I will demonstrate how we do this with some of the dates above, before inviting you to construct images for the remaining dates. We will then trouble-shoot some possible issues with memorising a string of dates, before discussing how to remember a 6-digit date of birth.

We will start with Mesmer's promotion of Animal

Magnetism. Our date is 1774. That gives us Ariana Grande (17) and the action of sword-fighting (74). I will locate the scene by the school cupboard where my Science teacher used to keep all of the magnets. The image to be remembered is Ariana Grande sword-fighting with Animal (from the muppets). To add to the scene, Animal is using a giant stereotypical U-shaped magnet to deflect Ariana's lunges.

I am sure you would have no trouble encoding the other dates, but let's choose one more for good measure.

This time around we will memorise 1954 as the date that Abraham Maslow helped to found *Humanistic Psychology* and later developed his famous Hierarchy of Needs. The date of 1954 gives us Paul Hardcastle (whom I always picture as some random DJ I once saw at a disco) eating from a trough! This unusual scene is taking place at the very top of the Great Pyramid in Giza. However, this pyramid is made up of people. Specifically, various psychologists and psychology students I have known. Recalling the pyramid would almost certainly make me think of the *Hierarchy of Needs*. The fact that the pyramid is formed of humans, not bricks, reminds me of Humanistic Psychology. And the strange sight of Paul Hardcastle eating from a trough gives me the date of

1954.

I would encourage you to go through the rest of the list and create your own images. Of course, you are not obliged to. You can simply move on to the next section, but you would only be selling yourself short. I would argue that you owe it to yourself to prove just powerful your memory really is. Besides, take it from this geek, it's a whole lot of fun!

Trouble-Shooting Historical Dates

All done? You did do it, right?

Assuming that you did go on to memorise the other 14 dates from our list, one problem you may have encountered is the repetition of the number 19. If you were using the characters from my list, that's an awful lot of Paul Hardcastles!

Now, that is not an insurmountable problem. After all, a DJ injecting himself with heroin is not too similar to a DJ playing cricket. Nevertheless, it may be more memorable it we could vary our images a little. The good news, is that there are three ways we could do this.

Firstly, we can group all of the 20th century dates together. For example, I have a museum that I use for my historic dates. In that museum, anything that took place in the 20th century is located on the same floor. I can also then place them in order on a journey round that floor, allowing me to not only learn the exact dates, but their relative flow in history.

Secondly, again if we use a wealth of 19s as our example, you can symbolise the 19 in some way. Instead of having a plethora of Paul Hardcastle's, we might employ other Deejays (Jon Peel, Howard Stern, Grandmaster Flash, etc.). Or we could use a turn-table in the background of each scene to remind us that it took place in 19-something or other. Simply placing some chunky headphones on someone's head might work!

Finally, we can solve the problem with 19s, by recognising that many of the dates we want to remember will take place between 1000 and 1999. We might then want to consider dropping the 1 altogether, at least from those dates that we know fall within that millennium. (We can usually decipher, from the event, if it fell within that time-period.) One way to do this is to place the 1 at the *end* of the digits. Therefore, 1974 becomes 9741 and 1836 becomes 8361. You will still face some repetition (namely 11, 21, 31, etc.), but it would almost certainly be less troublesome than too many Paul Hardcastles!

Specific Dates and Personal Info

When a client gives us their date of birth, it is likely going to translate into a 6-digit number. For example, 16.07.74. Of course, it might be 17.05.01. However, we do not need to worry about adding the 4-digit century, as the age of the client in front of us will make clear whether we are dealing with 1901 or 2001!

Using the 6 digit Person-Action-Person encoding we have discussed previously, 16.07.74 would become Alan Sugar pointing a pistol at Gerard Depardieu. If I wanted to recall that this was the birth-date of Chris Pontius (US actor and *Jackass* cast member), I would simply combine my new image with whatever I used to link Chris' name to his face. (In my judgemental eyes, Chris Pontius has quite wide nostrils. So, I would probably combine this with a donkey – well, an *ass*, actually! – pontificating whilst dressed as the Pope!

(In our final chapter, on Memorising Personal Information, I will reveal the whole system I use for memorising dates of birth and connecting that with all of the other client data you may want to recall.)

Let's look at one more example. Bruce Lee was born on November 27th, 1940. That is, 27.11.40. This converts into the memorable image of Bob Geldoff spinning around

Dominic O'Brien. This one is fairly easy. The location becomes the stair-case scene in *Game of Death* where Bruce Lee fights Kareem Abdul-Jabbar. However, although that may be happening in the background (at least, within ear-shot, where I can hear Bruce's familiar yells), the scene I focus on is Bob Geldoff spinning Dominic O'Brien around as if he was a spinning-top. Sure, Bruce's battle was more epic, but that is just as memorable in my book!

Using the 6-digit date of birth format, you will naturally find that you are dealing with a limited number of months. There will only ever be 12 months to choose from, which gives us a limited series of actions to imagine. One way round this is to vary how you encode them. On one occasion you might use the 2-digit number from our Person-Action list. However, the next time round you could use the number (1-12) from an extended number-rhyme or number-shape system. And so on.

Using Your Body as a Memory Palace

If you are ever caught without a journey and need one immediately, you can always use the one you carry with you everywhere. The human body is perfect for the task!
I will provide a basic list, explain how to use it and then offer an extended version. It is worth familiarising yourself with both.

- Top of your Head
- Eyebrows
- Eyes
- Ears
- Nose
- Mouth
- Neck
- Shoulders
- Chest
- Stomach

- Upper Arm
- Forearm
- Hand
- Thigh
- Knee
- Calf
- Foot
- Toes

That gives us 18 distinct locations to use. You will notice that in the basic list, I do not distinguish between sides of the body. In fact, when it comes to the eyes, I even imagine wearing glasses, so that I can focus on both eyes at once. My reasoning is simply that this enables me to speed through the body (in this version) and not have to worry about remembering which side I am focusing on.

So, let's imagine we are aiming to memorise the books of Richard Nongard. The impressive list includes the following:

1. Advanced Parallel Programming
2. The Seven Most Effective Methods of Self-Hypnosis
3. Turn Around Trauma
4. Real Hope

5. The Step Spouse

6. Reframing Hypnotherapy

7. Expert Hypnosis Scripts

8. Viral Leadership

9. Counselling People who have killed other people

10. Speak Ericksonian

11. Transformational Leadership

12. Contextual Psychology

13. Magic Words in Hypnosis

14. Big Book of Hypnosis Scripts

15. Medical Meditation

16. Medical Hypnotherapy

17. Keys to the Mind

18. Inductions and Deepeners

The basic idea will be familiar to you by now, so I will simply give you the 18 images I use. It helps that I know these books, so I am able to encode each title in a fairly basic image. If you were aiming to recall the full title for a book you did not previously know, you may need to add more to the images I've used.

1. Top of Head

Advanced Parallel Programming

I envisage parallel train tracks nailed to the top of my head. Along each track are sat a series of computer Programmers.

2. Eyebrows

The Seven Most Effective Methods of Self-Hypnosis

Brad Pitt (playing his character from the movie Seven) is lying comfortably on my admittedly substantial eyebrows, having hypnotised himself into a pleasant trance.

3. Eyes

Turn Around Trauma

My glasses are playing the music video for the song Total Eclipse of the Heart, by Bonnie Tyler. Conveniently, that song includes the lyric, 'Turn around, bright eyes.'

4. Ears

Real Hope

One of my ears is home to a long dangling ear-ring, made from a piece of fishing line (which makes me think of a fishing *reel*). Hanging from the fishing line is an ornate photo of Bob Hope.

5. Nose

The Step Spouse

A Bride and groom are sat on each nostril, like they are door-steps, facing away from each other.

6. Mouth

Reframing Hypnotherapy

This is slightly easier for me as I am currently sporting a rather dashing goatee beard. A professional Picture Framer is working on my beard, to fashion it into the perfect frame for my mouth.

7. Neck

Expert Hypnosis Scripts

My neck has been pierced as if I have to received a tracheotomy. Instead of blood, ink, letters and words come *spurting* out.

8. Shoulders

Viral Leadership

With some displeasure, I see Boris Johnson coughing and spluttering on my shoulder, as he announced to the nation that he has caught the Coronavirus.

9. Chest

Counselling People who have killed other people

I imagine receiving a tattoo of various famed mass murderers across my chest. However, the tattoo is not taking place in a proper studio, but on a therapist's couch.

10. Stomach

Speak Ericksonian

I squeeze my ample belly so that it looks like a mouth across my belly button. I then manipulate the sides of the mouth and hear Milton Ericksonian saying, "That's right!" (Feel free to picture your belly, not mine, for this one!)

11. Upper Arm

Transformational Leadership

My upper arm is made of machine parts and looks as if it belongs on the set of one of the *Transformers* movies. The arm is yellow with a black stripe, reminding me of *Bumblebee*.

12. Forearm

Contextual Psychology

Sat on my forearm are a row of teenagers engaging in

a texting contest. Seriously, it was a thing on British TV for a while!

13. Hand

Magic Words in Hypnosis

I open up my hand to see a black top hat in my palm. Just as I go to pick it up, out jumps a white rabbit!

14. Thigh

Big Book of Hypnosis Scripts

I imagine struggling to walk with a big book wrapped all the way round my thigh.

15. Knee

Medical Meditation

I am kneeling to meditate and finding it incredibly painful. A friend of mine who is a nurse then shows me a far more comfortable and sustainable position.

16. Calf

Medical Hypnotherapy

I imagine my calf being shaved to prepare me for a medical procedure, having injured my leg from too much walking.

17. Foot

Keys to the Mind

I simply envision an enormous locked door in the middle of my foot, that I put a key in and open.

18. Toes

Inductions and Deepeners

I count each of my toes, backwards from 10 down to 1, taking myself into a nice hypnotic state as I do so.

As you will have noticed, sometimes I zoom in on the

body part and imagine it like a landscape. Sometimes I view the action through my own eyes, or as if I am part of the scene. At other times, I use an action that the body part might carry out (such as kneeling) to place the image.

At first, it may seem as if your body parts will not make reliable locations, but I assure you they can. For some unknown reason, before beginning this book I really did learn Richard Nongard's books in that way (according to Amazon, that is the order they were published in) – and I can easily recall the list to this day.

One thing that surprised me was how much more effective it was if I touched the body part both during the memorisation and when later recalling the list. However, this makes complete sense if for no other reason than that multi-sensory memories seem more reliably recalled than others. Give it a go and see for yourself!

Extending the Body Method

Obviously, the body parts you use can be lessened, or increased as needed. To be most reliable, I would recommend sticking to the same parts each time, so that you do not miss one out during recall. However, if you have a short version and a long version, that would not be an issue.

A longer version could include both sides of the body, each individual finger and toe, even the back of the body if picturing buttocks is appealing to you! Lynne Kelly offers the following parts, providing a journey with 35 locations:

1. Right hand
2. Right wrist
3. Right forearm
4. Right elbow
5. Right biceps
6. Right shoulder
7. Right ear
8. Top of my head
9. Eyes
10. Nose
11. Mouth
12. Chin
13. Left ear
14. Left shoulder
15. Left biceps
16. Left elbow

17. Left forearm

18. Left wrist

19. Left hand

20. Neck

21. Chest

22. Stomach

23. Backside

24. Left thigh

25. Left knee

26. Left shin

27. Left ankle

28. Left foot

29. Left toes

30. Right thigh

31. Right knee

32. Right shin

33. Right ankle

34. Right foot

35. Right toes[20]

Kelly then uses her palm, fingers and the back of her hands for facts related to astronomy. All rather

---

20 Lynne Kelly, Memory Craft, pp. 130-131.

impressive, but perhaps beyond our needs at this point![21]

A further way to extend the Body method for locations is to use someone else's body. The most effective way to do this is to pick bodies that are distinct in some way. So, for example, picturing The Incredible Hulk's Chest will look very different to picturing Superman's, which will also be quite different to Wonder Woman's!

Incorporating people who have specific and easily identifiable outfits could even provide extra locations if so desired. For example, you could include Superman's cloak, Iron Man's chest, Batman's belt and so on. The key here would be using exactly the same parts each time you picture that person, so that you have a reliable and memorable number of locations.

You may even want to categorise the bodies you use. For example, you could have ten super-heroes, ten athletes, ten musicians and so on.

Just don't blame me if someone asks what you're thinking about and you have to explain why you are focusing on Thor's buttocks!

---

21 Ibid, pp. 133-135.

Names & Faces

Social Amnesia?

It is extremely common to forget someone's name the second we hear it. Meredith is introduced as "Meredith Bakslavich." We are told a few facts about her. She talks for a little bit. Then someone else joins the conversion and we have to introduce her. Dammit! What was her name?!

For some reason, we have almost trained ourselves not to pay attention when someone is giving us their name. It seems to be the Person equivalent of looking at our watch and not really seeing what time it is. Nothing else that I share in this chapter is more useful than the following four words: Do not do that!

Show an interest in their name. Maybe ask what it means, its ethnic background, how they spell it, etc. You can hardly go wrong here, as people generally love to be asked about themselves.

Then, repeat their name. If you do this too often it is

obvious. Yet, you can always get away with using their name immediately.

"This is Meredith."

- "Nice to meet you, Meredith!"

Finally, use their name when you say goodbye. As well as being good manners, this further helps cement the name in your mind. They were introduced by means of their name. You showed an interest in their name. Now, when they leave, you "book-end" the conversation by using their name as you say goodbye.

Where have I seen you before?

Have you ever noticed that when you cannot remember someone's name the first thing you often think is, "where do I know them from?" Yet, if we manage to place them somewhere, we might find all of the information we once knew about them comes straight back to us.

This is why the first piece of advice I would give to you if you are aiming to remember names and faces is to place someone in a location. It is one thing to remember their face, or their name, but our aim is to link the two. Locating the memory somewhere not only helps to add to the link, but it also provides an extra level of organisation to the association.

So, if you meet someone and they give you their name, transport them to a location that they bring to mind. For example, if they remind you of someone, you can picture them at that person's house, or at their place of work, or even somewhere you regularly met them. Or, you might locate this person at their own workplace, if you happen to learn their occupation along with their name.

Alternatively, their name itself might conjure up a location. For example, anyone called Roger might make you think of Roger Federer and therefore bring to mind a tennis court. All Justins may provoke thoughts of Justin Timberlake and be pictured on a dance-floor.

Caricature Their Features

This stage can involve stereotyping, exaggerating and pretty much insulting someone. However, you will be keeping it to yourself, so I would not worry too much about that!

Exaggerate those ever so slightly pointy ears and let them bring to mind Mr. Spock. Notice their cavernous nostrils and think of someone caving there. Make their cheeks stand out like ski slopes. If they have bright blue eyes, turn them on like lights, or sparkling gems. And so on.

Associate an Image With Their Chosen Name

It can save a great deal of time and effort if you have some prepared images that you always employ. For example, anyone named James might make you think of James Bond and thus by symbolised by a gun. Any Dwayne's might make you think of Ayers Rock.

I would recommend, as with the numbers, to always rely on your own images. However, for those names that do not bring anyone to mind, you might want to check-out Ron White's extended list that I've included as an appendix.

Family Names

When it comes to Family names, things can be a little more complicated and may involve more stages. Some Family names will have automatic meanings. For example, Snow, Banks or Whitefield.

Then there will be names with familiar associations. These include names like Hanks, Bourne, or Nixon.

Finally, some names will have no obvious association. These will need to be artificially created. This step usually involves unpacking names. Examples might include Baldwin, which could be turned into 'bald one' or 'bald win.' Van Nuys becomes 'van noise.' Bakslavich might become 'back slap itch,' or even 'back slave itch.'

As with the Chosen names, you might want to employ set images for common prefixes and suffixes. Examples some people recommend include an egg or oven for the suffix ova, the Sun for son, or a hamburger for the prefixes Mc, Mac or Mack.

Linking Names and Faces

The final step is associating the names image with the feature we earlier caricatured. This will almost always be a facial characteristic. However, it could be an unusually high-pitched voice, short stature, or so on.

Here is an example, using Meredith Bakslavich, whom we met earlier.

The name Meredith sounds like "Merry dish" to me.

That makes me think of a childhood visit to one of the *Happy Eater* chain of restaurants. In the restaurant, I see them crouched over, reminding me of their bad posture. However, they seem to be crouching for a good reason. Strapped to their back is the escaped slave Django itching their head.

If I could not remember Ms. Bakslavich's name on our second encounter, I would naturally try to place them. I would then recall the location, which would give me their first name - "merry dish." When I picture Meredith at the Happy Eater, I will see her crouching and see the slave on her back itching her head.

Imagine you meet someone who looks a lot like a friend of yours. Then when they tell you their name is James Chinaski, you use the name to create a key image that you then place with the person in your friend's house.

You might have the person holding a gun and spinning around like at the beginning of a James Bond movie. When you take a closer look at them, you see that there is a large key stuck in their beard - "chin as key."

Summary

This may all seem rather complex and convoluted, though I would suggest it becomes almost second nature after a while. Let's look at what is taking place in the steps we have used.

To begin with, where possible, we locate them somewhere. This step will be practically automatic.[22] You are doing a couple of thing at this point. Firstly, you are observing them. You are not just looking at their face or repeating their name to yourself. Instead, you are taking in their entirety, allowing yourself to notice and become aware of whatever they bring to mind.

Secondly, you are acknowledging a subconscious association. You may not even be aware why James Chinaski reminds you of your friend, yet that is where your mind goes. There is every chance your mind would go there again the next time you met them (unless you had focused on something transient such as an item of clothing). So, accept the association and go with it.

Thirdly, by locating the memory somewhere, you are organising and making use of our brain's apparent

____

22 If you are meeting someone somewhere unique, you can just use that initial meeting point. However, for example, if you are learning client's names it will be less effective if they are all met in your clinic.

tendency to 'find' spatial memories more easily.

Then you observe and pay careful attention to their face, or other stand-out features. You can then expand on these to make their face even more memorable.

The next step is converting their name(s) into a more memorable image. We can do this by using pre-defined images, which often works better for common Chosen names. Or we can do it by unpacking their Family name and creating a sort of story to link the two.

Finally, we link the memorable name image with (usually) a memorable facial feature and place them in the location.

So, with all of these steps, what we are effectively doing is:

1. Noticing them as a person
2. Observing their face
3. Become acquainted with their name
4. Linking the name with the face with the person

In short, we are paying attention to someone, to the effect they have on us, the memories, feelings and associations they bring to mind. Then we are focusing on and remembering their face. Then we do exactly the same with their name, spending as much time 'looking' at it as we do looking at their face. Finally, we associate the name and the face and organise them by placing them in a location.

Not all of these steps are vital and some of them will happen automatically with some people you meet. However, given that some of us are better at observing and recalling visual data, whilst others are more suited to noticing and recalling auditory data, this is the most holistic, reliable and durable technique I know of for remembering names and face. And, more importantly, people!

Star Signs and Months of the Year

The information in this chapter is provided purely to demonstrate some of the principles we are discussing. I personally have no interest in astrology, though some of my clients do.

The dates for the signs of the zodiac can vary slightly every year. However, generally speaking, they change around the 19th to the 23rd of every month. So, if you wanted to simply know the rough dates for a specific Star Sign, you could use this little trick: If you add two to the number of the zodiac sign, you get the month it begins. For example, Aries is the first sign. Adding 2 to that gives us the 3rd month. So, we know Aries must begin between March 19th and 23rd.

Pisces is the 12th sign. 12+2=14. We know there are only 12 months, so that must mean Pisces begins in the 2nd month, which is February.

For that trick to work, you would need to know the order of the signs. A simple way to learn them is to remember the following mnemonic:

> All the great constellations look very lovely;
> shining stars creating animal patterns.

Yet, in all honesty, the method for learning the signs and their exact dates is so simple that I see no reason to avoid it.

Make Associations between Sign and Month

It will not surprise you by now to know that I remember the signs of the Zodiac by associating the star sign with its month. I am sure it will also not surprise you to know that we do that by converting both the sign and the month into images.

Converting the Star signs is easy as each sign already has a symbol, most of which are readily recognisable. However, for those that are not, I have provided some suggestions below.

Aries – Ram

I think of – be patient with me here! - an 'airy Ram!

Taurus – Bull

I think of a Tourist to Spain trying to get in to take photos of a Bull-fight.

Gemini – Twins

This is a difficult one for me to offer an association for, because it is so naturally already embedded for me. If you think of "Gemini" and don't picture the twin symbol, the following associations could work.

"Jem and I..." - simply conjure-up a scene involving you and your twin, in this case being someone called Jem.

"Gems..." Perhaps picture two twins you know (or famous twins you easily think of) stealing precious gems.

A combination of these two images might involve either someone you know named Jem (Jen would work), or one of a pair of twins (better if they are identical). Then simply imagine that their eyeball, or at least their iris, has been replaced by a precious jewel. Get it? "Gem in Eye."

Cancer – Crab

I am afraid that the association I make here is extremely weak. (I did warn you that it is best to make up your own!) I simply think of Cancer as a disease that eats up healthy cells... like a crab!

Leo – Lion

Well, that's too easy to comment on.

Virgo – Virgin / Maiden

This will already be memorable to most people. You could picture John Virgo playing snooker with the Virgin Mary though, just for added effect.

Libra – Scales

This one is another personal one, but I think it might be intuitive for others too. When I think of Libra I think of Library (which comes from the Greek word for book, *Libre*). For some reason, I then think of dusty books about Law and other such topics. My mind then makes the leap to the Scales of Justice.

However, there's no reason you couldn't imagine a scene like a Librarian weighing the books you are taking out of the Library and charging you accordingly.

Scorpio – Scorpion

This is just so easy that it's getting silly now!

Sagittarius – Archer

With apologies to him, I picture Robin Hood with a saggy bottom! You could just as easily combine sage (the herb, or the wise sayings) with someone who has the surname Archer, or even with the drink.

Capricorn – Goat

Officially, the Goat that symbolises Capricorn is a Mountain Goat. So, I picture a capricious goat wearing the sort of cap that I imagine someone climbing mountains would wear.

Aquarius – Water-bearer

It really does not take a lot of imagination to remember that AQUArius is connected with water in some way!

Piesces – Fish

This sounds like "Pie Seas" to me, so I let that conjure up an image of a hot Fish Pie.

So, hopefully it won't take any real effort on your part to make those associations. I suspect that you would not even need to read back through that list to recall them, in fact.

Memorising the Dates

We now have a symbol to represent each star sign. That symbol will be doing something in the scene we create. It will give us our Action. The action therefore symbolises the Star Sign.

Each month will suggest a certain location. For example, December is in front of a large xmas tree. February makes me think of valentines day and thus romance, so it conjures up the Eiffel tower.

Finally, the date on which each sign begins is converted into a person. So, we have a Person (representing the date) performing a specific Action (symbolizing the sign) in a particular location (which gives us the month.

So, with no further ado, here are the images I use to recall the dates of the signs of the Zodiac:

Aries (21st March – 20th April) : Mr T. is riding a hairy ram ('airy ram) into a marching band

Taurus (20th April - 21st May) : Bo Derek is taking photos of people in a joke shop

Gemini (21st May - 21st June) : Mr T. is digging for gems in the House of Commons

Cancer (21st June - 23rd July) : Mr. T is crawling sideways like a crab on a sand Dune. He is sweating in the heat due to the weight of the gold around his neck

Leo (23rd July - 23rd August) : Jesus Christ is roaring like a Lion at Julie's house!

Virgo (23rd August to 23rd Sept.) : Jesus Christ is dressed as the Virgin Mary blessing people as they flow past on a chocolate river

Libra (23rd Sept. to 23rd Oct.) : Jesus Christ is weighing books at the foot of the twin towers

Scorpio (23rd Oct. - 22nd Nov.) : Jesus Christ is running away from an attacking scorpion at Nursing home

Sagittarius (22nd Nov. to 22nd Dec.) : Boris Becker is shooting arrows into the sky at a Fireworks show (in lieu of fireworks!)

Capricorn (22nd Dec. to 20 Jan.) : Boris Becker is butting his head, like a Capricious goat, onto a large Xmas tree

Aquarius (20th Jan. - 19th Feb.): Bo Derek can be seen spilling an enormous barrel of water (which she had optimistically been trying to carry on her shoulders!) in the middle of a very busy department store (during the January sales)

Pisces (19 Feb. - 21st March) : Paul Hardcastle is fishing off of the top of the Eiffel tower!

Using this system could hardly be any easier. Asking "who is doing this action in this scene?" gives you the day of the month the Sign begins.

Asking "where are they doing it?" gives you the month.

The benefit of this approach is that if I can only think of the sign/action, I can ask where it is happening. That thereby gives me the Star sign and the month.

If I want to know what sign occurs in which month, I

just go to the location for that month.

Memorising the order of the Calendar

The following information is completely superfluous. For some readers, this will be totally unnecessary. However, some might find it interesting or useful, so I am including it any way.

Pretty much everyone knows that January is the 1st month and December the 12th. As a result of this, most people can remember that February is the 2nd and November the 11th.

Yet, have you ever had to briefly pause to figure out that April is the 4th month, or July is the 7th? If so, you may find the following quite interesting.

Would it be useful to instantly know that, for example, the 6th month is June? I think it would and the good news is that there are a host of ways to learn that.

We could symbolise the months and then just associate each symbolised image with one of the peg words from e.g. the Number Rhyme method.

Alternatively, we could simply devise a new 12-stage journey, placing each month's image at the appropriate stage. However, I like to use a different approach, which entails associating each month with a completely different event and image. It may take some extra work to memorise this new list, but I have found it useful and I enjoy the extra knowledge it gives me.

Basically, I have memorised a key fact associated with every date that corresponds to the month. So, that would be January 1st, April 4th, July 7th and so on.

I now automatically associate these events with the month and as such instantly know the number and order of the months.

Jan 1 - New Year's Day

This is easy. I just think of New Year's Day sales - and shudder!

Feb 2 - Original valentines day

Valentine's Day was originally on February 2nd. This is a fairly easy association, as Valentine's Day is generally thought of as a day for couples. Or, I might recall that Feb 2nd is Groundhog Day in the US. This reminds me of the movie where events kept repeating (i.e. happening a second time, at least!).

March 3 - End of the Miners Strike

March 3rd, 1985 was the end of the historic Miner's Strike in the UK. I remember this as the day the miners "marched" free, though that's not exactly what happened!

April 4 - MLK

April 4th is famously the date that Martin Luther-King was assassinated.

May 5th – Cinco de Mayo

This is one of those dates that is easy if you know it. May 5th is the Mexican festival of Cinco de Mayo, which literally means May 5th.

June 6th - D-Day

June 6th is the anniversary of the landing of the Allied Forces in Normandy, known as D-Day.

July 7 - Bombing in London

July 7th is the date of the 7/7 bombing of buses in Central London.

Aug 8 – 8888

August 8th, 1988 was the date of (what became known as) the 8888 uprising in Burma.

Sept 9 – Mary Queen of Scots

Mary Queen of Scots coronation took place on 9/9 when she was 9 months old!

Oct 10 – World Mental Health Day

October 10th is widely recognised as World Mental Health Day.

Nov 11 - Remembrance Day

November 11th is known in many countries as Remembrance Day, or (in the US) Veterans Day.

Dec 12 – Numerous!

For some reason, I seem to know a few facts related to December 12th. It is, for example, Bruce Springsteen's birthday. Additionally, December 12th, 1963 is when Kenya (formerly British East Africa) declared independence from the UK. Finally, Dec. 12th 1965 is the date of the last concert the Beatles played in England.

You might want to learn your own historical facts for information for the relevant days. However, I recommend this as a relatively pain-free and interesting way to remember the numerical order of each month.

When I think of August, I automatically think of the 8888 uprising in Burma, meaning I know that August is the 8th month. October is associated in my head with an outdated and stereotypical asylum, reminding me that World Mental Health Day is on October 10th.

This is perhaps all completely unnecessary, but I enjoy knowing these 12 extra dates and at some point in my life I hope to meet someone who is as impressed by my knowledge of them as I am!

How to Memorise 100 Digits of Pi

100 Digits of Pi is a fairly pointless thing to memorise. If you're interested in competitive memory, it is not even close to being impressive.[23] And if you're not, why would you even bother?

However, it may function as a useful demonstration of what is possible with a well-trained memory. If you can easily memorise 100 digits of an abstract number, there is no real reason you cannot remember mobile phone numbers, credit card numbers, how many of my books you still need to write reviews for and on and on...

So, without further ado, here are the first 100 digits of Pi:

3.1415926535897932384626433832795028841971693993751058209749445923078164062862089986280348253421170679

I suppose that to most people, with no awareness of

---

23 The current World Record stands at 100,000 digits.

memory tools, that would seem like an impossible, ridiculous and pointless thing to do. Thankfully, having read this far, you know that at least one of those beliefs is untrue!

As we are dealing with numbers we will employ simple Person-Action imagery. So, that will involve breaking-up the 100 digits into groups of 4:

```
1415 9265 3589 7932 3846 2643 3832 7950
2884 1971 6939 9375 1058 2097 4944 5923
0781 6406 2862 0899 8628 0348 2534 2117
0679
```

Hopefully, by now you look at a number like that and do not feel as daunted as you once may have done. In fact, all we will need to do now is come up with a simple 25-stage journey. If I was doing this in a hurry, perhaps as a memory demonstration, I suspect that I would use one of my 26-stage journeys that I have for memorising packs of cards. Alternatively, I would use the Alphabet system to devise a journey, as discussed previously.

However, ideally, I would recommend using an educational journey. I would think of a Library, Museum, College, University or School building. As always, this works far more effectively if you come up with journeys that are *meaningful to you*. So, I would advise putting this book down, creating a 25-stage journey and coming back.

If you are insistent on using my journeys, here is a route through an imaginary school using the Alphabet System.

1. Algebra (Obviously, the Maths room – good start!)
2. Biology (Science Lab where the skeleton is)
3. Chemistry (Science in front of Periodic Table)
4. Dance Hall
5. English Classroom (at the front)
6. French
7. Geography
8. History
9. I.T. Suite
10. Journalism (back of English classroom)
11. Karate (Gym, at the front)
12. Lunch Hall
13. Metal work room
14. Needlework
15. Orchestra (Music Room)
16. Physical Education (Gym, by the ropes)

17. Q (Canteen, i.e. Queue!)

18. Religious Studies

19. Science Teacher's Desk

20. Textiles Room

21. University!

22. Violins (Careful not to mix with 15!)

23. Water Fountain

24. X (Nurse's office, i.e. X-ray, eczema, etc.)

25. Youth-work (Mentor's Office)

26. Z (The Library, where we got our Zzzzzs in!)

Some of these might not work for you. It's also possible that you might mix-up e.g. L and Q and O and V. (If there was more than one potential problem with a letter, I would advise changing something. However, we are doing this quickly to demonstrate ease-of-use!)

Now, going back to our Person-Action list, I would memorise the first 100 digits of Pi with a simple 26-stage journey like this:

1. Algebra (Obviously, the Maths room – good start!) - 1415 = Arthur Daley experimenting with test tubes

2. Biology (Science Lab where the skeleton is) - 9265 = Nora Batty feeding a crocodile

3. Chemistry (Science in front of Periodic Table) - 3589 = Clint Eastwood looking through telescope

4. Dance Hall - 7932 = Gamal Nasser missing the ball and falling over

5. English Classroom (at the front) - 3846 = Charlton Heston frying a pancake

6. French - 2643 = Bart Simpson pulling a rabbit out of a hat

7. Geography - 3832 = Charlton Heston missing ball and falling

8. History - 7950 = Gamal Nasser pinning tail on donkey

9. I.T. Suite - 2884 = Benny Hinn falling and cracking open

10. Journalism (back of English classroom) - 1971 = Paul Hardcastle throwing a grenade

11. Karate (Gym, at the front) - 6939 = Sam Neil chopping wood in half

12. Lunch Hall - 9375 = Neville Chamberlain dances latina

13. Metal work room - 1058 = Tony Blair fishing

14. Needlework - 2097 = Bo Derek drinking beer

15. Orchestra (Music Room) - 4944 = David Niven flying

16. PE (Gym, by the ropes) - 5923 = Ed Norton being crucified

17. Q (Canteen, i.e. Queue!) - 0781 = James Bond juggling

18. Religious Studies - 6406 = Steve Davis playing Bridge

19. Science Teacher's Desk - 2862 = Benny Hinn playing golf

20. Textiles Room – 0899 = Oliver Hardy washing up

21. University! - 8628 = Homer Simpson pushing forehead

22. Violins - 0348 = Olivia Cooke flapping like a mermaid

23. Water Fountain - 2534 = Billy Elliot begging for more gruel

24. X (Nurse's office, i.e. X-ray, eczema, etc.) - 2117 = Mr. T singing into a microphone

25. Youth-work (Mentor's Office) - 0679 = Omar Sharif building a pyramid

26. Z (The Library, where we got our Zzzzzs in!) - Me celebrating by eating a lot of Pie!

Yes, it may initially take you 10 or 15 minutes to memorise. And, sure, it is completely pointless. Yet, seriously, how cool is that? You just easily learned the first 100 digits of Pi!

Remembering Client Intake Details

I will now demonstrate a system that easily enables you to remember the following 11 valuable points of client information:

- Their name
- Their occupation
- Date of birth
- Their phone number
- Their partner/spouse
- Their children's ages
- The issue they have come to see you for
- Relevant historical data
- Their primary goal
- Their main motivations
- Their hobbies / leisure pursuits

If we cannot agree that such information – easily remembered and recalled – is worth the price of this book then I am really doing something wrong!

None of what follows will be new to you if you have read through the book to this stage. We are simply bringing together the various techniques and using a rather unique location to place them all in.

Let's start there...

The Location

The location we are going to use to reliably remember our Client's Accurate Record is a CAR! Bear with me. This will make sense in a moment.

The type of car will depend on a number of factors, including the amount of detail you need to remember. After all, someone with 6 children will need a bigger vehicle than someone with none!

Additionally, some people may just scream a certain type of car at us. If I was working with a professional athlete, I would most likely imagine a sportier car than someone working in a suburban accountancy firm. Or if I was working with a Mr. Attenborough, I might use a safari -ready jeep, something worthy of an explorer, or anything that made me think of their namesake.

Information is recorded in the Car in the following

ways:

Driver's Seat

This is where I place my client. I dress them in such a way as to remind me of their occupation, if they have one. On their left shoulder, I place their date of birth and on their right I put their phone number.

I employ their face to recall their name.

Passenger Seat

Sitting in the Passenger seat is the client's partner(s), if they currently have one. I usually dress them in such a way as to remind me of any pertinent details. For example, a wedding outfit if they are newly married, or about to be. If they are deceased, I may picture them as a ghost, in a coffin, or similar. If there is an ex whom it is significant to recall, I have them sat there split in half.

Generally, it is not necessary to remember too much about a partner or spouse, unless I am working with a couple or family. At most, their existence and perhaps their name will suffice.

Back Seat

Any children are placed in the back seat(s). I do not personally tend to memorise more than their gender and their age, unless their name is especially relevant for some reason.

Obviously, the number of children in the back seat reflects how many children the client has. I then use the Number encoding we have previously learned to remember their age. However, if the client had a 13-year old daughter, it would not do to simply picture Al Capone, as that would lead me to think of a son. So, the options are to either picture a stereotypical 13-year old girl, dressed as Al Capone. Or to see Al Capone somehow adjusted to make him represent a female (e.g. wearing what might traditionally be considered a very feminine dress).[24]

Back Window (the view behind)

Out of the back window – as if I am using the window like a TV screen – I see something to represent the issue

---

24 The best options here for speed or memorisation and recall are to unfortunately make use of stereotypes. You also need to consider what works for your list of characters.

that they have come to see me for.

The Boot / Trunk

In the boot, I place images that represent anything the client has brought up from their past that they – or I – feel is significant. This may not actually be the case, but it is worth being aware of the information, even if just to highlight that the client feels they are still "stuck" in the past in some way.

Front Window (the view ahead)

Looking out of the front window, I see their goal, preferred future, or where they hope to get to. Most of my work incorporates Solution-Focused Brief Therapy, so this information is usually essential to my sessions.

As with the back, I use the front window as if it is a movie screen that I am viewing their future upon.

Dashboard

On the dashboard, usually in miniature, I place various images or scenes that remind me of my client's motivations. These can be things like health (an ambulance), children (a baby), money (a pile of coins), religious beliefs (a cross, or relevant symbol) and so on.

Glove Compartment

In the glove compartment are images or symbols – again often in miniature – that represent my client's hobbies or leisure interests. These can vary enormously, but frequently found items include a football, paintbrush, bike, record player, condoms, wine glass, running shoes, TV set, and a spider monkey! (The latter reminds me of the TV show *Friends*, as socialising with friends is of course how many people choose to spend their free time.)

Putting it All Together

It will be helpful to look at an example or two of this in practice. I will provide the client details and then share the way I encode the information to make it more memorable.

CASE STUDY 1

Name: Tanya Edwards

Date of Birth: 30.07.87

Phone number: 07833 812218

Occupation: School Teacher

Partner: Mike

Children: Daughter 8. Son (Max) 12.

Issue: Feels guilt over affair in past, through which she got pregnant with Max

History:
- Tanya's father also had an affair
- Mike used to be friends with the man she had an affair with. He no longer makes friends
- It took Mike "years" to forgive her.

Goal: to forgive herself - to feel free to love herself

Motivation(s):

- thinks will help her love Max more

- be happier

- that *she* would be less jealous of mike

- to enjoy physical intimacy again

- Mike could make some new friends.

Interests:

- Singing

- Education

- Board games

- Camping

- Puzzles.

Hopefully, by now nothing that follows will surprise you. All I am doing at this point is applying what we have already covered in previous chapters.

The Car – Immediate Association

Tanya's car is a small family hatchback. However, from the outside, it is yellow in colour and resembles the stereotype of a School Bus that I saw in US movies as a child.

Driver's Seat – Name, DOB, Phone, Occupation

I zoom-in on Tanya's face. Along her prominent cheek bones, I see a very *tanned* Eddie "the Eagle" *Edwards* skiing.

On her left shoulder, I see Henry Cooper (83) riding a chariot (38). The chariot is pulling along a trailer that contains Alexander Graham Bell (12) who breaks a Snickers bar in half (21) and uses it as the nose for the snowman (8) next to him.

Meanwhile, on Tanya's right shoulder, Conan O'Brien (30) is pointing a pistol (07) at HG Wells (87).

As Tanya is a school teacher, she is dressed smartly but conservatively. She is wearing a lanyard and has a pen behind her ear.

Passenger Seat - Partner

I place Tanya's husband, Mike, in the passenger seat. As the marital relationship is relevant to our work together, I want to remember his name. So, I replace Mike's head with a giant vintage microphone.

Back Seats - Children

There are two back seats, to represent Tanya's two children.

There is a son, aged 12, named Max. He is dressed like a 12-year old Alexander Graham Bell. However, he also has a plush toy of Max, from Pokemon, as I felt that I needed to remember his name.

Next to Max (incidentally, Max is sat behind Tanya, not Mike) is Sophie, aged 8. She looks in every way like a typical 8-year old girl, except that she is dressed like Oliver Hardy! (I might have included a pet on a seat if it had seemed relevant)

Back Window – The Issue

When I look out of the back window, it is as if I am looking at a Cinema screen, playing a well-known scene from *Fatal Attraction* (a famous movie about an affair). However, when Beth lifts up the pot lid, it is not a bunny being boiled, but a doll. (I thought that actually picturing a baby in there might be a bit much!)

The Boot / Trunk – History

As Tanya's father also had an affair, I see a representation of my own father – his prized black and white wedding photo. However, in the photo, another woman's face has been stuck on top of my mother's head!

There is also a calendar to remind me of the time Mike took to forgive Tanya.

As Mike used to be friends with the man Tanya had the affair with, I see a Spider Monkey (to represent Friends) chewing on the head of a male action figure.

Front Window – The Goal / Preferred Future

Out the front window, I see a scene of Tanya in a confessional box. However, rather than a curtain, the confessional has bars. (There is no visible figure in the other side of the confessional, by the way, as this is not about anyone else forgiving Tanya.) As she bows her head, the prison doors fling open and Tanya steps out, forgiven and free.

Dashboard - Motivation(s)

I will merely list the items that are scattered on Tanya's dashboard, replacing the bobbly headed figures that often occupy such space.

There is a Big Mac box that contains a beating heart. A cuddly Cheshire Cat. A bowl of jelly. A pack of condoms. And there is also a microphone that is holding hands with a spider monkey.

You may prefer to link these items in some way, much as we did with the phone number and date of birth. However, I tend to simply picture them as if they are toys, statuettes or small stationary items of some kind.

Glove Compartment – Interests

In the Glove compartment we have: a statue of an Opera Singer (we cannot use a microphone to represent singing, as we are using that for Tanya's husband), a mortarboard or Oxford cap, a game of Snakes and Ladders, a tiny tent and a 3D wooden jigsaw puzzle piece.

With all of that very basic association, imagining and organisation, we have effectively shown how relatively straightforward and pain-free it can be to remember client details.

We will look at one more example to demonstrate this further.

CASE STUDY 2

Name: Emmanuel Oblunga

Date of Birth: 01.12.70

Phone number: 07902 678907

Occupation: Bus Driver

Partner: Has partner, but shared no information

Children, Boy 10, Boy 14, Boy 18, Grandson, 1 yr

Issue: Has recently developed fear of driving, so job is at risk

History:
- Had panic attack once when driving
- Mother was "always" very anxious

Goal: to drive confidently

Motivation(s):
- Job security
- Freedom
- Increased self-esteem

Interests:
- Golf
- Grandson
- Doing up a car

And here is how I would memorise this Client Accurate Record:

The Car – Immediate Association

This car is, predictably enough, a Minibus.

Driver's Seat – Name, DOB, Phone, Occupation

Obviously, I am placing Emmanuel in a Bus Driver's uniform. However, it is more like the sort of outfit worn by drivers in the 60s and 70s, complete with a peaked cap.

On the peak of the cap, I see one of my favourite scenes from the classic sitcom *Fawlty Towers*. In the first episode, *Manuel* is carrying a tray of butter. However, in my rendition of the scene, the tray is *oblong* shaped and on it there is a human brain, complete with brain stem including the medulla *oblongata*.

Emmanuel's left shoulder is the location for an unusual scene where Nick Offerman (90) rides a skateboard (26) into Goldie Hawn (78) as she is chopping wood (90). This nudges her and sends her axe (7) flying.

On his other shoulder, I see Orphan Annie (01) telephoning (12) George Orwell (70). Actually, she's speaking to him through a tin-can-and-string phone, but the picture still translates the numbers for me!

Passenger Seat – Partner

Merely to record that Emmanuel has a partner – and not to allow any confusion due to an empty seat – I place a red Love Heart cushion here.

Back Seats – Children

In the back, there are 4 bus seats, one of which contains a baby seat.

None of the children's names seem relevant, so I simply see 3 boys dressed like Tony Blair, Arthur Daley and Adolf Hitler. Hitler has his arm around the baby seat to remind me that the 1-year old sat in there is his.

Back Window – The Issue

In the back window, I see a scene from the movie Speed, with the bus passengers – and the driver! – screaming in fear.

The Boot / Trunk - History

The boot car contains a small toy wind-up car. When the car is wound-up, instead of driving along it simply shudders, as if shivering.

Also in the boot is a small doll of my mother, biting her nails.

Front Window – The Goal / Preferred Future

When I look out of the front window, I simply see

Emmanuel driving confidently. He makes "brmmm" noises as he drives with a ridiculously big smile on his face and his chest pushed-out with pride.

Dashboard – Motivation(s)

On the dashboard are a toy Security Guard, a pair of *open* handcuffs and a figurine of a King with his hands on his hips. (I had no idea how to symbolise self-esteem, so did an internet search for tattoos on the theme. The best I saw was of hands on a hip and a crown hovering above.)

Glove Compartment – Interests

The Glove compartment contains three simple items. There is a golf club, a baby's rattle and a toy sports Car that is battered and missing two doors!

Expanding the CAR

If you find that you need more from your CAR, there are a number of ways to create extra locations. The most obvious way to do this is to add items or symbols that indicate when you are to zoom-in for extra information. Here are some items that I use:

6-sided Die

I use a 6-sided die to remind me that I have added extra data using the number-shape method. I imagine lifting up the lid of the dice and jumping in. I then find myself in a scene involving a candle. From there, I move onto a swan and so on.

20-sided Die

If there is a 20-sided die – as often used in board games like Dungeons and Dragons – it tells me that I have employed the number-rhyme method up to 20. As I did with the 6-sided die, I lift the lid and jump into that scene.

Big Letter A

A big plastic letter A reminds me that I have made use of a 26-stage Alphabet peg system.

Map

If I ever see a map, it informs me that I have connected a whole journey to the CAR. The cover of the map will reveal the first location of the journey and let me know where to start from.

***

There you have it! You have just learned an incredibly easy way to remember vital client information. Of course, you are welcome to adapt and improve that – or any of the techniques in this book – and apply them to your needs as suitable. I would only ask that if you do so, drop me a line as I would love to hear about it!

258

What Next?

Is there a better Number-Letter system?

There are a number of ways that the system taught in this book could be improved. We have already spoken of expanding Person-Action (PA) to a Person performing an Action on another Person (PAP). However, even that can be extended.

It is possible – and relatively straightforward – to extend a Person-Action list into a Person-Action-Object list.[25] This simply involves assigning a specific object to each number from 00 to 99. So, using our means of converting numbers into letters, 22 could become Boris Becker (P) playing tennis (A) with a tennis racket (O).

The reason I do not do this is because I like the freedom of allowing my first Person to perform their action however they choose. For example, I might want Donald Duck to smash Charlton Heston over the head with an item that is found in the location. I do not want to

---

25 This is one of the methods favoured by many Memory Competitors.

limit the Person's action to the Object represented by the next 2 digits.

Additionally, I know that if a scene ends with an object, rather than a person, it is taken from the Number-Rhyme or Number-Shape systems and is therefore a single digit.

Of course, if you do choose to go down the route of devising a 99-objects list, a logical next step would be a PAOP system. That would involve a Person performing an Action with an Object upon Another person. That allows you to capture 8 digits in just one image!

Finally, there are different ways to encode numbers into digits. The method that was favoured before Dominic O'Brien became World Memory Champion was a system known as the Major System. This fell out of favour towards the end of the 20th Century, but then gained renewed fervour with a method adapted by Ben Pridmore.

Since then, others have returned to the Major System - often inspired by Ben and those who followed in his footsteps - and developed it even further.

For example, with the original Major System means of encoding digits, there was no specific word for e.g. 192. Instead that translated into T and P and N. This could give us the word 'tie-pin' or the phrase, 'ten pink ninjas.'[26]

---

26 Using the Major System, the following number-letter conversions take place:

Such flexibility may seem useful, even desirable. However, it has a downside. It provides more options for encoding the numbers in the first place. Yet, when it comes to recalling the number, you may have to consider every possible image or phrase that could represent the numbers 192.

For both speed and accuracy of recall, it is far more effective for 192 to translate into a specific word every time it is encountered. So, one of the advances promoted by the likes of Ben Pridmore and Alex Mullen is to use the Major System to develop a list of pre-defined images from 000 to 999.

Generally, those who use the Major System do not worry about adding Actions and Objects, as they do not limit themselves to people. Yet, even without that - and it remains a possibility - encoding 3 digits in one image would appear more effective than encoding just 2.

However, there is something we need to bear in mind here. You will already know this by now, but the most effective memory system is the one that is most personal to you.

For example, thanks to a teenage interest in Napoleon,

---

0 = z, s, 1 = t, d, 2 = n, 3 = m, 4 = r, 5 = l, 6 = j, sh , ch, soft g, 7 = k, q, hard c or g, 8 = f, v, 9 = p, b.

I will forever think of Napoleon Bonaparte whenever I see the numbers 1815. No encoding is necessary at all. Similarly, I will think of a Burmese friend of mine when I see 8888 and an old I.T. colleague of mine (who was overly concerned with the predicted 'millennium bug') whenever I see the number 2000.

So, can you imagine how effective it would be if it were possible to construct your own memorable list of all numbers from 0000 to 9999?

Nevertheless, for now, the means of converting numbers into letters recommended by O'Brien (which he humbly names the DOMINIC system!) is undeniably user-friendly. Thus, it is possible that its very simplicity is a key to its strength.

How Else Can I Apply This?

You might want to consider using the techniques taught in this book to learn:

- The order of US Presidents
- Kings and Queens of Great Britain
- The Plays of Shakespeare
- Lists of phobias and their definitions

- Foreign languages
- Developments within Cognitive Therapy
- Palmistry
- Facts related to major World religions
- DSM 5 (Diagnostic and Statistical Manual of Mental Disorders) diagnoses
- Capital cities of the World
- World flags
- Cloud formations and facts
- Birds native to South America
- Best Picture Oscar winners
- Astronomical data
- Etc.!

The list really is endless. However, I assure you that you now have in your hands the skills and strategies needed to memorise all of the above and more.

Other Useful Knowledge

I would recommend the books of Lynne Kelly to anyone interested in the history and application of memory techniques. They demonstrate the powerful and historically popular use of the method of loci. However, they also raise some interesting points regarding kinaesthetic memories.

As I mentioned when using your body as a memory palace, touching the various parts of your body seems to amplify the effectiveness of the technique. Similarly, actually physically walking round a museum whilst imagining items to be remembered would almost certainly be more powerful than merely picturing the stages of a journey around the same museum.

You may also find it interesting to research state-dependent learning and context-dependent learning. This is an area that I intend to write more on at a later date. So, feel free to do your own investigations and beat me to it!

What Now?

Well, only two things remain. Firstly, go back and actually *do* any of the exercises that you skipped. Secondly, <u>put this into practice</u>!

I am confident that as you begin to apply the principles and techniques taught in this book, you will discover just how valuable they are. Then, the more you use them in your daily life – both personal and professional – the more intuitive, effortless and effective they will become.

Have fun. And happy memories!

GRAHAM OLD

Bibliography

Baddeley, Alan D. *Your Memory: a User's Guide*. Carlton Books, 2004.

Buzan, Tony. *Master Your Memory*. BBC Active, 2006.

Buzan, Tony. *Speed Memory*. David & Charles, 1977.

Elman, H. L. *Blueprint of the Dave Elman Induction*. Dave Elman Hypnosis Institute, 2011.

Foer, Joshua. *Moonwalking with Einstein: the Art and Science of Remembering Everything*. Penguin Books, 2011.

Furst, Bruno. *The Practical Way to a Better Memory*. R & W Heap, 1977.

Furst, Bruno, and Lotte Furst. *You Can Remember! A Home Study Course in Memory and Concentration*. (Revised Edition.). Memory and Concentration Studies, 1967.

Hancock, Jonathan. *Jonathan Hancock's Mindpower System*. Hodder, 1996.

Higbee, Kenneth L. *Your Memory: How It Works and How to Improve It*. Paragon House, 2001.

Kelly, Lynne. *Memory Craft: Improve Your Memory Using the Most Powerful Methods from around the World*. Allen & Unwin, 2019.

Kelly, Lynne. *The Memory Code: the Traditional Aboriginal Memory Technique That Unlocks the Secrets of Stonehenge, Easter Island and Ancient Monuments the World Over*. Allen & Unwin, 2016.

Lorayne, Harry, and Jerry Lucas. *The Memory Book: the Classic Guide to Improving Your Memory at Work, at School, and at Play*. Prelude Books, 2017.

Lorayne, Harry. *Remembering People: the Key to Success*. Scarborough House, 1990.

O'Brien, Dominic. *How to Develop a Perfect Memory*. Headline, 1994.

Old, Graham. *The Elman Induction*. Plastic Spoon, 2016.

Pridmore, Ben. *How to Be Clever*. Lulu.com, 2013.

Yates, Frances. *The Art of Memory*. Penguin, 1966.

GRAHAM OLD

APPENDIX

Ron White's Extended Names List

I will blatantly steal Ron White's suggestions for images for the following common Chosen names.[27] This list is free from his website and should be considered a partial list:

Common Female names

Abby – A Bee

Abigail – A bee in a pail

Adele – A Bell

Alice - Lice

Allison – Lice in the sun

Amy – Aiming

Angie – Ants drinking tea

Ann – Ant

Anita - kneading

---

27 In some cultures, the Chosen name is known as the First name, or even the Christian name.

Annette – A net

Annie – Orphan Annie

April – A pill

Ashley – Ashes

Audrey – Laundry

Barbara – barbed wire

Beatrice – beat rice

Becky – horse bucking

Belinda – Bee in a window(winda)

Bernadette – burn a net

Beth – bath

Betty – betting

Beverly – bed of leaves

Billie – billy goat

Bobbie – fishing bobber

Bonnie – Bonnet

Brenda – bent window (winda)

Bridget – Bridges

Camille – camel

Candice- can of dice

Candy – candy

Carla – car with lace

Carmen – car and man

Carol – Christmas carol

Celeste – stars

Charlotte – spider web

Cheryl – chair that is ill

Chloe – clover

Chris – cross

Chrissy – cross in the sea

Christine – Christmas tree

Cicely – sis being silly

Cindy – cinnamon candy

Clara – clarinet

Claudia – cloud

Colleen – calling

Connie – convict

Crystal – crystal vase

Daphne – dolphin

Darlene – door with beans

Dawn – dawn

Debbie – dead bee

Deborah – dead boar

Denise – disease

Diana – dying ants

Dixie – Confederate flag

Donna – Donald Duck

Doris – doors

Dorothy – tornado (Wizard of Oz)

Dottie – dots shaped like 'E'

Edna – head saying 'ahh'

Eileen – eye leaning

Elaine – air plane

Eleanor – plane landing on door

Elise – A lease

Elizabeth – lizard breath

Ellen – island

Ellie – belly

Emily – family

Erica – ear

Eve – Christmas Eve

Evelyn - violin

Faith – church

Felicia – fleece

Florence – floor dance

Frances – Eiffel Tower

Gabrielle – Gabby (talking) bell

Gail – gale force wind

Georgia – gorge

Gina – blue jeans

Ginger – ginger bread man

Ginny – bottle of gin on knees

Glenda – blender

Gloria – Old Glory

Grace – saying a prayer

Hannah – hand

Harriet – lariat

Hattie – hat with an 'E'

Heather – feather

Heidi – someone hiding

Helen – light (what Helen means)

Holly – boughs of holly

Hope – rope, soap

Irene – eye ring

Iris – a wrist

Jackie – car jack

Jacqueline – lint on a jack

Jamie – chain on your knee

Jan – jam

Janet – jam in a net

Janice – jeans in a noose

Jeanette – jeans in a net

Jeanie – genie

Jennifer – chin fur

Jenny – chinny

Jessica – vest with cuffs

Jill – pill

Jo – sloppy joe hamburger

Joan – Joan of Arc

Joanne – sloppy joe w/ ants

Joy – Joy dishwashing liquid

Joyce – juice

Juanita – one knee

Judith – blue desk

Judy – chewing tea

Julie – jewelry

June – june bug

Karen – carrot

Kate – gate

Katherine – cat that runs

Kathleen – cat that leans

Kathy – cat

Katie – kite

Kay – key

Kim – swim

Kirsten – skirt with a stem

Laura – laurels

Laurie – lowering an 'E'

Leslie – less than sign '<'

Lillian – lily with ants on it

Lily – lily

Linda – window (winda)

Lisa – Mona Lisa

Lois – lost 'S'

Loretta – lower it

Lorraine – low rain

Louise – low easel

Lucille – loose sail

Lucinda – loose cinder

Lucy – I Love Lucy

Lynn – lint

Madeline – mad at lint

Mandy – mandolin

Marcy – marching

Margaret – market

Marge – barge

Maria – sangria wine

Marian – mare with ants

Marie – mare with an 'E'

Marilyn – marry lint

Marjorie – my jury

Marsha – marsh mellow

Martha – vineyard

Mary – merry go round

Marry Ellen – marry a melon

Melanie – melon on your knee

Melissa – molasses

Meredith – mare in a dish

Miriam – mirror ham

Mitzi – mitt that can see

Mona – moaning

Monica – harmonica

Nan – nun

Nancy – nun eating seeds

Natalie – gnats

Nellie – kneeling

Nicole – Nickel

Nora – snore ah!

Noreen – no rain

Norma – normal

Olive – olives

Olivia – oh liver!

Pam – spam

Pamela – panelling

Pat – act of patting

Patricia – pats of butter

Patty – hamburger patty

Paula – ball with an 'A'

Pauline – pole that leans

Peg – peg

Penny – penny (coin)

Phyllis – philly

Priscilla – pass the Jello

Rachel – ray shining on a shell

Ramona – ram moaning

Rebecca – reach for the deck

Renee – raining A's

Roberta – robot

Robin – bird

Rochelle – row of shells

Rosa – rose ah!

Rosalie – rose on your knee

Rosalyn – rosin (bag)

Rose – rose

Roxanne – rocks in hand

Ruth – Baby Ruth candy bar

Sadie – saddle

Sally – salad

Samantha – saw a man

Sandra – sander

Sandy – Sand

Sarah – Sarah Lee cup cakes

Sasha – sash

Sherry – bottle of sherry

Sharon – sharing

Sheila – shield

Sheryl – chair that is ill

Shirley – shirt sleeves

Sidney – sit on a knee

Sylvia – silver ware

Sonia – Sony Walkman

Sophia – sew a bee

Stacy – stay seated

Stephanie – step on knees

Sue – suit

Sue Ann – suit with ants

Susan – lazy Suzan

Susannah – snoozing

Tammy – tummy

Teresa – tree saw

Terry – terry cloth

Tess – test

Vanessa – van wearing a dress

Vicky – Vick's cough drops

Victoria – victory

Vivian – we win

Wanda – wand

Windy – wind

Yvette – Corvette

Yvonne – heave on

Zoe – sew an 'E'

Common Male names

Aaron – air gun

Abe – ape

Adam – a dam

Al – owl

Alan – alan wrench

Albert – burnt owl

Alex – owl that licks

Alexander – leg sander

Alfred – owl fried

Alonzo – bonzo (clown)

Alvin – owl wins

Andrew – ants drew

Andy – ants drinking tea

Angelo – angel eating jello

Anthony – ants in a tree

Archie – archery

Armand – arm band

Arnold – arm hold

Art – art work

Arthur – author

Austin – cowboy boot (Texas)

Barney – barn

Barry – berry

Bart – dart

Ben – bench

Benny – bending

Benjamin – bend a man

Bernard – St Bernard

Bernie – burn a knee

Bert – bird

Bill – duck's bill

Bob – bobsled

Bobby – bobby pin

Brad – bread

Bradford – bread in a Ford

Bradley – bread with leaves

Brandon – branded

Brian – brain

Brock – rock with a 'B'

Bruce – bruise

Bud – rose bud

Ceasar – Julius Ceasar

Cameron – camera

Carl – curl

Carlos – car that is lost

Carter – charter a boat

Cary – carry

Cecil – seal

Cedric – red brick

Chad – chaps

Charles – charcoal

Charlie – charred leaves

Chester – chest of drawers

Chet – Jet

Chris – cross

Christian – Christ

Christopher – kiss furr

Chuck – chalk

Clark – clock

Claude – cloud

Clayton – ton of clay

Cliff –cliff

Clifford – Ford going off cliff

Clint – lint

Clinton – ton of lint

Clyde – Clydesdale horse

Cole – coal

Colin – calling

Conrad – con(vict) rat

Corey – apple core

Craig – crack

Curt – curtain

Dan – dam

Daniel – van yells

Darren – da rent

Darryl – barrel

Dave – cave

David – divot

Dennis – dentist

Derek – oil derrick

Dick – deck

Dirk – dirt

Dominick – dominoes

Don – dawn

Donald – Donald Duck

Doug – dig

Douglas – dug a glass

Drew – drew

Duane – drain

Dunking – dunking

Dusty – dusting

Dwight – white 'D'

Earl – pearl

Ed – head

Eddie – eddy

Edgar – head gear

Edmund – head mount

Edward – head ward

Edwin – head wind

Eli – eel eye

Emmanuel – a manual

Eric – ear ache

Ernie – ear and knee

Erwin – ear & wind

Ethan – eating

Evan – oven

Everette – sever it

Felix – feel it

Fletcher – fetcher

Floyd – flood

Frank – frankfurter

Fred – fried egg

Freddy – frayed 'E'

Frederick – frayed brick

Garrett – chair it

Gary – garage

Geoffrey – chef in a tree

George – gorge

Gerald – chair that is old

Gil – fish gil

Gilbert – burnt fish gils

Graham – graham crackers

Grant – granite (rock)

Greg – keg

Gus – gust of wind

Hal – hail

Hank – han(d)kerchief

Hans – hands

Harold – hair that is old

Harry – hair

Hector – heckler

Herb – herb

Herbert – herb & bird

Howard – coward

Hugh – ewe

Irv – nerve

Irving – swerving

Isaac – eye sack

Ivan – eye on van

Jack – car jack

Jacob – Jacob's ladder

Jake – shade

James – chains

Jason – jaybird in the sun

Jay – jaybird

Jeff – chef

Jeffrey – chef in a tree

Jeremy – chair on me

Jerome – chair roam

Jerry – cherry

Jess – chest

Jim – gym

Joe – sloppy Joe (hamburger)

Joel – jewel

Joey – kangaroo

John – toilet

Jonah – whale

Jonathan – toilet that is thin

Jordan – jaw of tin

Jose – hose

Joshua – shower

Juan – wand

Jud – jug

Julio – jewel that is low

Justin – justice

Keith – keys

Ken – can

Kenneth – can on a net

Kent – tent

Kevin – cave in

Kirk – kick

Kyle – tile

Lance – Sir Lancelot

Larry – lariat

Lawrence – law for ants

Lee – leaves

Len – lens

Leo – lion

Leon – lean on

Leroy – leaves on a toy

Les – less than sign '<'

Lionel – Lionel train

Lou – blue (color)

Lucas – low kiss

Luke – luke warm water

Luther – roofer with an 'L'

Lyle – aisle

Mack – Mack Truck

Manny – man with an 'E'

Mark – marker

Marshall – law enforcement

Martin – Martian

Marvin – carving

Mason – mason jar

Matt – door matt

Matthew – matt in a pew

Maurice – more rice

Max – mix

Maxwell – mix well

Mel – melon

Melvin – melt van

Michael – bicycle

Mickey – Mickey Mouse

Mike – microphone

Miles – miles

Mitch – mitt

Morris – Morris The Cat

Morgan – organ

Nathan – gnat in your head

Ned – bed

Neal – nail

Nick – nickel

Noah – no air

Noel – Christmas Noel

Norman – Norseman

Oliver – olive

Oscar – Academy award

Otis – Otis elevator

Owen – rowing

Pat – pat something

Patrick – St Patrick

Paul – ball

Pedro – paid to row

Pete – Pete Moss

Peter – Peter cottontail

Phil – fill up

Pierre – pier

Preston – pressing a ton

Quincy – wind and sea

Ralph – raft

Randall – ram and doll

Randolph – ram and dolphin

Randy – bottle of brandy

Ray – ray of light

Raymond – ray on a mound

Rex – wrecks

Richard – wrench in a yard

Richie – dollar sign

Rick – brick

Rob – robber

Robbie – robe

Robert – robot

Rod – rod

Roderick – rod in a brick

Rodney – rod in knee

Roger – rod in chair

Roland – rolling

Ron – rum

Ronald – Ronald McDonald

Ronnie – running

Ross – boss

Roy – Roy Rogers

Russ – rusts

Russell – rustle

Sam – Uncle Sam

Sammy – Uncle Sam on knee

Samuel – Uncle Sam on mule

Sandy – sand

Scott – Scott paper towels

Shawn – yawn

Seymour – see more

Sheldon – shielding

Sherman – German shepard

Sid – sit

Stan – stand

Steve – stove

Stewart – steward

Stu – stew

Tad – tadpole

Teddy – teddy bear

Terry – tearing an 'E'

Tex – Texas

Theodore – see a door

Thomas – thermos

Tim – tin can

Timothy – tin of tea

Toby – toe and bee

Todd – toad

Tom – tom cat

Tommy – Tommy gun

Tony – Tony the Tiger

Tracy – tracing an 'E'

Ty – tie

Tyrone – tie rowing

Tyler – tire

Van – van

Vince – fence

Vern – fern

Vernon – furry nun

Vic – Vick's cough drop

Vincent – mint fence

Wade – wade in pool

Wallace – walrus

Walt – waltz

Walter – wallpaper

Ward – ward

Warren – warden

Wayne – rain

About the Author

Graham Old is a Solution-focused Hypnotist from the United Kingdom. A Graduate of Spurgeon's College, London and the University of Wales, Graham is a former University Chaplain and Community Pastor and remains an active participant of local peace and justice campaigns. He has experience as a Father's Worker and Assistant Social Worker, as well as working in private clinical practice and running one of the most popular hypnosis sites on the web.

Graham is a popular conference speaker, writer and trainer, with over twenty-five years experience teaching meditation and self-hypnosis. He is an insightful presence in contemporary hypnosis and the developer of the acclaimed *Therapeutic Inductions* approach.